M000294000

21st CENTURY BURNING BUSHES

21st CENTURY BURNING BUSHES

Volume I: Spiritual Burning Bushes

Dr. Setrag Khoshafian

21st Century Burning Bushes: Volume I: Spiritual Burning Bushes

Published by 21st Century Burning Bushes

Copyright © 2023 by Dr. Setrag Khoshafian
All rights reserved. Neither this book, nor any parts within it may be sold or reproduced in any form or by any electronic or mechanical means, including information storage and retrieval systems, without permission in writing from the author. The only exception is by a reviewer, who may quote short excerpts in a review.

Library of Congress Control Number: 2023940689

ISBN (hardcover): 9781662939891
ISBN (paperback): 9781662939907
eISBN: 9781662939914

To Silva Khoshafian (1952–2021).
An amazing woman of God and my soulmate for forty years.
Silva enriched and blessed my life as well as the life of countless
many—with her Christ-centered, selfless dedication to her family,
her friends, and her ministry through sharing the Word with
wisdom and compassion, especially for women's ministries.

Heaven is enriched by her presence.

Strength and dignity are her clothing, and
she laughs at the time to come.
—*Proverbs 31:25*

The Lord has granted us forty years of bliss and blessed us
with amazing four sons, Nishan, Jonathan, Shahan and Nareg;
three daughters in love: Jennifer, Courtney and Aline; and
three grandchildren: James, Joelle and Joshua.

The book's artwork was done by Semaline Betarian.

I am thankful that the Lord bestowed divine inspiration upon the artwork, and I appreciate how Semaline helped bring it to fruition.

Contents

Preface to Burning Bushes

T he Burning Bush incident in Exodus[1] set the course of mankind's history: the relationship of God with humanity. It is one of the most unique and important dynamics between the Creator and His creation. Yet it started with the initiative of a man—Moses— who saw something strange and took the initiative. When he did, the Creator responded, and the rest is history.

There have been and continue to be other Burning Bushes that are amazing, wonderful, sometimes strange, and even alarming or fearful. There are many *21st Century Burning Bushes* that need to be followed and analyzed to hear the voice of the Creator and what He is communicating to us. There are so many that it took me four volumes to cover them in twenty-one chapters!

All Burning Bushes reflect amazing dynamics between us and the Creator.

These Burning Bushes are pointing to the conclusion and culmination of history.

The book series will attempt to cover the entire spectrum of strange, amazing, unusual, and profound phenomena. It will also cover what looks routine yet with layers of depth and profound ramifications.

It is a "living book" series—where there will be a QR code at the end of chapters to extend and update the content and engage the readers.

The twenty-first century is full of contradictions. There have been huge scientific and technological accomplishments. Yet the last two centuries have been full of amazing scientific discoveries, devastating wars, total moral collapse, monetary meltdowns, and even slavery. The twenty-first century is a century that is witnessing a return of paganism and strange areal phenomena. It has also witnessed an unprecedented sharing of the Gospel. Are these the precursors to the return of our Lord? Most likely. The signs and

---

[1] Exodus 3:1–17.

wonders and Burning Bushes are addressed in the four volumes as follows:

- *Volume I: Spiritual Burning Bushes.* The current volume, volume 1, and its foundation will cover the Burning Bushes that are essentially spiritual: the Lord Jesus Christ, the Word, revivals, and supernatural manifestations. This is where it all starts—there are blessings and challenges with huge consequences for humanity and our relationship with the Creator. We expand on volume 1 below.

- *Volume II: Science and Technology.* The twenty-first century is witnessing an explosion of scientific discoveries and digital technological applications. This second volume will delve into the scientific and technological trends that are transforming society, especially Gen Z. For the first time, we are starting to see how automation and AI are replacing human labor and transforming society. Quantum mechanics has transformed our understanding of the very nature of the universe— with particle characteristics that appear metaphysical. The twenty-first century also witnessed the emergence of digital currencies and digital social networks that have transformed society. There is an explosion of sophistication in humanlike robotics with advances in AI that are constantly seeking artificial sentient intelligence. Also, there are serious efforts by the military around the world to create Humanity 2.0—also known as Transhumanism. At the same time, Darwinian theories are challenged on all scientific (genetic, cosmic, archaeological) fronts through new discoveries that have validated Intelligent Design as a much more viable objective scientific explanation, shaking the very foundation of the materialistic worldview.

- *Volume III: Culture, Morality, and the Kingdom.* Scientific and technological advances, though almost magical, have also left a huge vacuum in the human soul. The twenty-first century is witnessing unprecedented and huge cultural and societal transformations—not all for the better. Throughout centuries, we have witnessed unprecedented collapses in morality, especially through wars, genocides, and abortions.[2] While some are attempting to control entire societies through the banner of saving the environment, there is a real possibility of nefarious plans to control

---

[2] http://www.earnestlycontendingforthefaith.com/AbortionTheBloodyFacts.html

humanity through a One World Government or a New World Order—with Orwellian agendas. Christians are becoming persona non grata: in businesses, educational institutes, and governments. The twenty-first century saw the emergence of a "woke" and anti-Christian culture dominated by extreme LGBTQIA+ and transgender agendas. In parallel, there is resurgence of heathen practices through New Age and Paganism. Some see it as a return to heathen practices—even glorification of Satan in entertainment and society at large. Yet there is another Divine Kingdom with its own system and hierarchy. This volume will cover angels and how He has used them—and continues to do so throughout history. Two kingdoms and two worldviews at war for the very soul of humanity.

- *Volume IV: Signs and Wonders—the End of Times*. This is the culmination of the Burning Bushes. While many of the Burning Bushes are also End-Times Burning Bushes, this volume delves into "fringe" topics such as Unidentified Flying Objects (UFOs or UAPs), megalithic structures, giants, and the Nephilim. We are witnessing the potential emergence of a new hybrid race through nefarious abductions and pregnancies! There are signs and wonders in the skies, on earth, and in supernatural manifestations that are also unprecedented. This chapter also covers the role of the state of Israel in end-times prophecies, especially through the interpretations of the prophetic books Daniel, Ezekiel, the book of Revelation, and others. The last chapter is about the New Heaven and New Earth: the ultimate Burning Bush and the culmination of history.

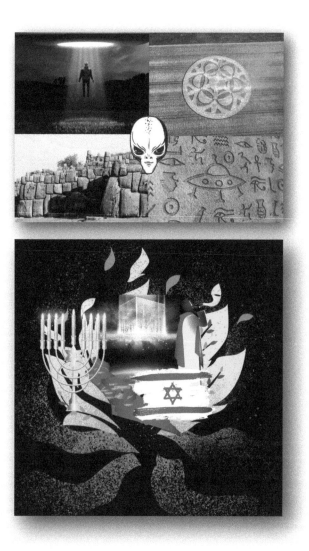

My prayer is that the Lord will encourage you to take notice of these Burning Bushes and have a personal relationship and revival within your own spiritual journey.

Do not ignore these Burning Bushes.

As you read the chapters in these volumes, prayerfully with as much intense interest as possible, consider what each Burning Bush is about. Do not discount them. Some are amazing. Others might be scary or worrisome. But they are all unusual. You need to show interest and resist apathy!

That is your part.

Responding and manifesting Himself and communicating with you is His part. He has never failed anyone and is eternally faithful and reliable!

On with the First Volume: *The Spiritual Burning Bushes*

This first volume sets the overall tone of the subsequent Burning Bushes. God is Spirit, and He has created us as spiritual beings—intended to have fellowship with Him. We are alive only if His Spirit lives within us, and that can only be achieved through a spiritual birth. Hence, the spiritual context of Burning Bushes is key.

It starts with the Burning Bush principles and perspectives. That is the foundation of everything unusual, exceptional, and even miraculous. Those who are true seekers will approach the Burning Bush uncovered in each chapter with an open mind. The most important spiritual Burning Bush is our Lord Jesus Christ. He is *amazing*! No wonder so much effort is exerted by the enemy to discredit Him. We shall address those. The second most important spiritual Burning Bush is the Word of God. In fact, Christ *is* the Word. The continuous bestseller and the most important book in history has been attacked and discredited. The book's resilience *and* impact on the lives of millions of Christians are manifestations of its Burning Bush qualities.

The last two chapters in this first volume is about revivals and supernatural gifts. The history of the Church is the history of revivals. Each revival is different, and every revival is itself a Burning Bush—amazing, wonderful, and unexpected. It is the ultimate *spiritual* Burning Bush as, by definition, revivals are the manifestations of the Holy Spirit. Increasingly, the Church has become naturalistic, yet the work of the Holy Spirit is often accompanied by supernatural manifestations and gifts. Occasionally, these are exhibited in the context of revivals. The last chapter is about the supernatural Burning Bushes—including the gifts of the Holy Spirit.

Living Book

The volumes of *21st Century Burning Bushes* are "living" books. This means I will be providing videos, additional content, and updates for each of the chapters of the series. Each chapter will have a QR code that could be scanned. The scanning will take you to a Burning Bushes website landing page for additional material for the specific chapter or topic. Here is the QR code for the volume series:

This is the QR code for this volume, *Volume I: Spiritual Burning Bushes*.

1. The Burning Bush

1.1.   Introduction

In Exodus 3:1–3 (NKJV) we read:

> Now Moses was tending the flock of Jethro his father-in-law, the priest of Midian. And he led the flock to the back of the desert, and came to Horeb, the mountain of God. And the Angel of the Lord appeared to him in a flame of fire from the midst of a bush. So he looked, and behold, the bush was burning with fire, but the bush was not consumed. Then Moses said, "I will now turn aside and see this great sight, why the bush does not burn."[3]

This was the start of Moses's calling to free the people of Israel. What is often overlooked is the fact that it was Moses who saw the amazing sight and turned aside to see what it's all about.

He (that is, Moses) took the initiative.

Initially God did not call him to come over. God manifested the great sight. Moses went to it. He could have ignored it and continued herding his sheep. History would have forgotten him. Instead, he turned aside.

This is the vital theme for all the chapters of this book.

It was unexplained, miraculous, out of place, unusual—you name it. But it was Moses who went to investigate what it was all about. Just imagine if he had ignored it and went about his business tending the flock. He would have missed the greatest calling of his life and the life of God's people!

This book series is about the unexplained, the unusual, the miraculous, the terrifying, the horrific, the signs that are all around us—all amazing Burning Bushes.

We have a choice. Will we turn aside and examine what these Burning Bushes mean? Or will we retire in the comfort of the

---

[3] Unless otherwise specified, most references from the Bible will be in the New International Version, https://www.biblegateway.com/versions/New-International-Version-NIV-Bible/

familiar—in our bubbles? I like the way NLT[4] puts it: Moses stared in amazement. Though the bush was engulfed in flames, it didn't burn up. "This is amazing," Moses said to himself. "Why isn't that bush burning up? I must go see it."

There are many amazing sights all around us.

Like the contractions and pangs preceding the birth of a child, their number and frequency is increasing.

Are these precursors to the Second Coming of our Lord Jesus Christ?

Perhaps. Most likely. Every age thought they were the last one.

Whatever they are, it is our duty to turn aside and examine the amazing sights. This book is a journey to stare in amazement and then seek as much as possible the *21st Century Burning Bushes*.

We cannot afford to be apathetic, cold, or even worse, lukewarm! We need to heed, pay attention, and act when needed. That is why each chapter will have practical recommendations for its Burning Bush.

As we shall see, some of these Burning Bushes have been around for centuries—even millennia. Nevertheless, in the twenty-first century, their fire, brightness, and frequency are increasing. It is critical for us as believers and for churches to be aware, prepared, and amazed. They all point to the nature and character of our Lord Jesus Christ. They are all a precursor to the final showdown.

Even agnostics or atheists cannot ignore these Burning Bushes.

1.2.   All Types of Burning Bushes

Moses's experience of the amazing Burning Bush was a positive one. It launched his prophetic calling and freed the people of Israel from slavery.

---

[4] New Living Translation, https://www.biblegateway.com/versions/New-Living-Translation-NLT-Bible

However, not all Burning Bushes are positive. There are "signs of the times" that precede doomsday predictions. In fact, many Burning Bushes discussed in the four volumes can be considered "negative" or at least cautionary for the coming end of times and the ultimate war that has been going on for millennia.

There are also others that are amazing in reflecting the glory of God our Creator. Therefore, the Burning Bushes covered here will be of different kinds and implications.

1.3.   Why This Book

Why a book series on *21st Century Burning Bushes*? There are four main reasons why this book series is written and, in fact, necessary for the coming years. Many renowned Christian authors and intellectuals ("giants" of faith) have written about several of the topics covered here. I am grateful and, in many ways, stand on their shoulders. They paved the way for this work. However, what I have tried to do is explain and join these Burning Bushes almost like connecting the dots in a puzzle. We are living in a wonderful universe that is at the same time in turmoil. The times we live in feel strange, to say the least. Who would have predicted COVID-19, the many wars the United States and other countries got dragged in, the cultural changes from transgender to woke culture? Add to that space exploration and scientific discoveries especially in quantum mechanics that are challenging our understanding of the laws of physics, at the very least.

1.3.1.   Prepare for the Second Coming of Christ and the End of the World

We are living in a unique time in history. Not to be too sensational, in 2023, the Doomsday Clock was ninety seconds to midnight. Here is a description of this apocalyptic measure from the scientific community:[5]

---

[5] https://thebulletin.org/doomsday-clock/current-time/

Founded in 1945 by Albert Einstein and University of Chicago scientists who helped develop the first atomic weapons in the Manhattan Project, the Bulletin of the Atomic Scientists created the Doomsday Clock two years later, using the imagery of apocalypse (midnight) and the contemporary idiom of nuclear explosion (countdown to zero) to convey threats to humanity and the planet. The Bulletin's Science and Security Board in consultation with its Board of Sponsors, which includes 11 Nobel laureates sets the Doomsday Clock every year. The Clock has become a universally recognized indicator of the world's vulnerability to catastrophe from nuclear weapons, climate change, and disruptive technologies in other domains.

From a Christian perspective, there have been many predictions for the end of times and the return of our Lord Jesus Christ. Each generation considered itself the last generation—the one just before the return of our Lord and the prime candidate of the rapture of the Church (if you believe in the rapture).

1.3.2. Admire the Wonders of God's Creation

We are living in a wonderful yet turbulent universe. Even as a *fallen* (more on that later) universe, wonders are all around us:[6]

> The heavens declare the glory of God;
>
> the skies proclaim the work of his hands.
>
> Day after day they pour forth speech;
>
> night after night they reveal knowledge.
>
> *(Psalm 19:1–2)*

But we also have a responsibility:

> Since what may be known about God is plain to them, because God has made it plain to them. For since the creation of the world God's invisible qualities—his eternal power and divine nature—have been clearly seen, being understood from what has been made, so that people are without excuse. (Romans 1:19–20)

---

[6] James Webb image from *The Atlantic*, https://www.theatlantic.com/photo/2022/07/first-images-from-the-james-webb-space-telescope/670489/

So, several of the topics will cover the wonders of the world around us—from what has been observed in the macro world through modern telescopes to what is being discovered in the subparticle world, especially the wonders of quantum mechanics.

1.3.3. *Relevance of the Gospel in the Twenty-First-Century Culture*

Many times, the Church has been guilty of presenting the gospel message in "Christianese": using language and terms that are familiar only to those who have grown up in Christian homes or have been attending church for a while. Also, our topics have become repetitive, with hardly any sermon or Bible study that addresses difficult and relevant topics, especially to the younger generations.

This loss of relevance often impacts the children of Christian families. Imagine a young man or woman raised in a Christian home going to Sunday school every Sunday, attending a Christian high school, and then going to a liberal college. The unchallenged messages of the Bible and the biblical narratives as well as the very foundations of the Christian faith will be challenged and attacked on all fronts. Many lose their faith in especially liberal colleges that are increasingly predisposed to certain anti-Christian belief and worldview systems.

It's akin to being exposed to new viruses for which they have no prior encounter or immunity. Their intellectual, mental, and spiritual immune system may not be equipped to fight off the infection of the pseudo-intellectualism that has infected most campuses. The result has often been devastating. Many young Christians, having been raised in Christian homes and church communities, suddenly realize they were living in a bubble.

Given the current challenges and attacks, the Church has often gone in a defense mode without addressing the difficult questions through profound and scholarly treatments. While the Burning

Bushes series is not an apologetics, we shall occasionally delve into robust treatment of difficult topics without shying away from the difficult challenges.

This happened to my children, and we had the best of intentions. We simply did not prepare them enough ("vaccinate" them, to use a more current term). There are topics from evolution; to science in general; to cultural trends such as sexuality, transgenderism; to more esoteric topics that are also becoming mainstream, such as Unidentified Flying Objects (UFOs [which are now renamed Unidentified Areal Phenomena [UAPs]).

The Church is silent on these topics by and large.

We should never compromise. Yet we should always be wise as serpents and relevant while remaining innocent as doves. No stone and no topic should be left unturned. If it is difficult, strange, challenging, or amazing, it is a Burning Bush.

So, we analyze it, go deep into it, and see what it is all about. Above all, we do not avoid or ignore it.

Replace *Jews* or *those outside the law* with *Millennials, Gen Z, Gen X*:

> To the Jews I became as a Jew, in order to win Jews. To those under the law I became as one under the law (though not being myself under the law) that I might win those under the law. To those outside the law I became as one outside the law (not being outside the law of God but under the law of Christ) that I might win those outside the law. To the weak I became weak, that I might win the weak. I have become all things to all people, that by all means I might save some. (1 Corinthians 9:20–22)

To become all things to all people, we need to understand what they are exposed to, what they are hearing and seeing, and what is the worldview that is surrounding them. It is not all negative. But whatever it is, we need to go deep into the Burning Bush with the ultimate goal of bringing a salvation message that is on target and relevant.

1.3.4.   Prepare for the Coming War: Be Aware and Counter the Different Deceptions and Techniques of the Enemy

Being relevant is important. But we also need to realize we are at war. From secret societies to the New Age, to woke culture, to trends toward One World Religion and One World Government—the pieces are coming together for an ultimate showdown.

Christianity is revolutionary. As the late Dr. Francis Schaeffer[7] stated:

> One of the greatest injustices we do to our young people is to ask them to be conservative. Christianity is not conservative, but revolutionary.

As we shall see, the other side (the kingdom of the enemy that has started with the lies and deceptions in the Garden of Eden) is shrewd and is preparing for war. The Christian side is mostly divided, with the majority engaged in "conservative," "classical," or "traditional" topics and interests, and letting the enemy completely change the narrative and trends of society, government, and churches to their end: the ultimate battle. A deception is being cooked, and the target is nothing less than the minds and souls of humanity – especially the believers.

---

[7] https://www.thegospelcoalition.org/article/know-your-evangelicals-francis-schaeffer/

1.4. Who Is the Target Audience?

Who then is the target audience of the book series?

The Burning Bushes book series provides a broad spectrum of topics. Some of these topics are related. Others seem quite different and strange but still are *implicitly* related. The best way to think about this is a country (more appropriately, a Kingdom) that is also at constant war. Many agencies need to operate and periodically cooperate for the well-being and protection of the Kingdom.

There are many departments and units within the agencies. Though they seem quite different, they do often interact and intersect (for example, think about the local police, the CIA, and the FBI—chasing various activities of a notorious international cartel—each with their own investigations).

Some of the topics (perhaps most) in the book series might sound irrelevant and not imminent or necessary for our day-to-day lives—for His Kingdom. If you peruse the very many wonderful sermons (now almost all online each Sunday), you will notice many common themes. They are mostly "safe" topics that rarely touch upon the content or topics covered here—"fringe" or outside-the-norm topics. However, the well-being and protection of the Kingdom does require us to pay attention: to watch for *all* the Burning Bushes.

The Lord is the Creator of this incredible universe we live in. He has provided—created or allowed—these "strange" sights all around us. It is up to us to turn aside and see what they are. None is accidental, and each plays a role in the Kingdom.

So, in a very real sense, the book series is intended for those Christians who are members of the Heavenly Kingdom—to operate as His citizens with different roles, depending upon the talents, gifts, responsibilities, and abilities the King has given them. Citizens of all levels—pastors, lay leaders, gifted believers—will all benefit from the book series. Each chapter will be followed with recommendations in the specific area and references for deeper studies and analysis. The book series is a tool for the Church and even unbelievers to appreciate the amazing universe we live in and then take action that leads to worship, repentance, or deeper walk with the Lord. We, as Christians, exist to enjoy Him and glorify Him. Let us seek His glory in the Burning Bushes.

The book also targets agnostics and atheists or nominal Christians who "feel" something is not right, and political as well as religious leaders who are not addressing the challenges that are degrading society. Each one of us has an emptiness we are trying to fill. I know, as I was an agnostic and I have been there. Here is how the French mathematician and philosopher Blaise Pascal[8] puts it:

> What else does this craving, and this helplessness, proclaim but that there was once in man a true happiness, of which all that now remains is the empty print and trace? This he tries in vain to fill with everything around him, seeking in things that are not there the help he cannot find in those that are,

---

[8] https://en.wikipedia.org/wiki/Blaise_Pascal

> though none can help, since this infinite abyss can be filled
> only with an infinite and immutable object; in other words
> by God himself.

There will be Burning Bush topics that address some of the causes and remedies of the emptiness and meaninglessness. It can help you address the objections of which deep down you know there are answers.

The book series attempts to provide a scholarly treatment of difficult Burning Bush topics. We shall provide plenty of examples that challenge core Christian beliefs. Yet we shall also delve deep into the amazing Burning Bush in each one of those. So, I request that you keep an open mind as we explore into topics that could be very relevant for you—from the fringe topics, to science, technology, and manifestation of supernatural or extra natural events.

The book is intended for all those who would like to connect the dots and see how all these Burning Bushes are converging—perhaps even guiding us in the meaning and culmination of history. Our Creator is encouraging us to turn around and see what they are all about and how they are all connected. It is much more than "end-of-times" signs, though we shall definitely address those. Some of these Burning Bushes have fires that have been burning for ages. It is time we pay some attention.

1.5. Categories of Great and Strange Sights

The Burning Bushes book series will cover a variety of topics aggregated in four volumes.

Some Burning Bushes are more current for the twenty-first century—such as AI, digital technologies, and an explosion in scientific discoveries, especially with the emergence of quantum mechanics. Others have been around for a while, such as the very nature of our Lord Jesus Christ and the Word. There are several topics that, on the one hand, are "strange"—incomprehensive and amazing—and at the same time can be considered a defense to our Christian faith.

Some Burning Bushes have seen a resurgence in recent years by *some* Christians. There are many topics that evangelical churches— traditional, mainline, or charismatic—will not touch (though we are seeing some exceptions to these). Interestingly, the Catholic Church has been ahead of the game in some of these topics. The Protestant and Orthodox churches—with few exceptions—also lag. Example topics here include UFOs/UAPs, giants, megalithic structures, and strange manifestations in the unseen realm. These are sometimes characterized as "fringe" topics.

We are also witnessing a resurgence of heathenistic beliefs and practices as well as indisputable One World Government and One World Religion trends to control societies.

The signs leading to the return of our Lord Jesus Christ are Burning Bushes *par excellence*! In fact, all the Burning Bushes can be considered signs pointing to the culmination of human history. The Lord Jesus gave *many* signs for His return in Matthew 24. We should take the totality of the great and strange signs together—to draw us nearer to the Lord, prepare us for the ultimate battle, and wait eagerly for His return. These will intersect directly or implicitly the prophecies in the Gospels, the book of Revelation, the book of Daniel, the book of Ezekiel, and others. There are many "birth pangs" Burning Bushes.

The four volumes will group and categorize the Burning Bushes. We start with *The Spiritual Burning Bushes* and Moses's initial interaction with God in volume 1 and culminate with the *Signs and Wonders—The End of Times* Burning Bushes in volume 4.

1.6.   Point, Counterpoint, God-Point

I love the quote credited to the seventeenth-century theologian Rupertus Meldenius: "In essentials, unity; in non-essentials, liberty; in all things, charity."

Over the centuries and especially most recently, Christians who are regenerated and Christ-centered while agreeing on the essential tenants of the Christian faith[9] have taken particularly divisive positions against one another. They have sometimes accused positions or doctrines that do not agree with theirs as "heretic," even though the doctrine or position itself does not impact one's salvation. Examples include interpretations of the book of Revelation or eschatology in general. Sadly, I have witnessed divisions and splitting of churches on nonessential theological points and on personalities.

The position in the book series is to elucidate the point-counterpoint on topics related to Burning Bushes but, above all, provide the *God-Point*. This can be illustrated through a triangle, and its inspiration comes primarily from the marriage relationship dynamics between a husband and wife. Every marriage goes through difficulties and misunderstandings. We are different. After all, *Men Are from Mars*

---

[9] I particularly dislike the term "Fundamentalist" as it has been used pejoratively meaning "unscientific, narrow-minded, judgmental, self-righteous, closed-minded, and even implicitly racist" or worse. I hold dearly to all the basic tenants of the Christian faith, and to the best of my abilities, I am none of these. I also know many regenerated Christians who are like me.

and Women Are from Venus.[10] Now, as the husband (point) and the wife (counterpoint) get closer to God (God-Point) on the triangle, they get closer to each other. The closer to God (hopefully, equally close), the closer to each other. I have learned this from my own marriage. Even after four kids, we enjoyed going to Christian couples' retreats to take some time off and get closer to God and to each other.[11]

There are many similar topics. Often Christians find themselves swept away by "packages" of issues or topics whose agenda is set forward by political or social organizations—not through the Christ-centered biblical perspective.

I often find it confusing why one must select being anti-abortion and anti-trans and at the same time, at best, be marginal on poverty, minorities, racial or environmental issues vs. pro-choice, together with all the liberal causes. In fact, this goes hand in hand with what is called cancel culture. There are many social justice issues and causes and issues that I agree with, especially when it comes to poverty and equality for women and minorities. The Bible says plenty about the poor and social justice and we shall cover these in volume 3. However, sexual orientation does not qualify one to be in the same category as a racial minority. One is a racial identity endowed by the Maker. The other could lead to a sinful lifestyle choice.

In her women's ministry, Silva helped hundreds of women in their physical, psychological, and spiritual struggles. She did her best to lift them up in every way she can, especially the widows and those who had lost their sons to war!

There is an interesting God-Point in James 1:17:

> Religion that God our Father accepts as pure and faultless is
> this: to look after orphans and widows in their distress and
> to keep oneself from being polluted by the world.

---

[10] Title of Dr. John Gray's book on understanding the opposite sex, https://www.amazon.com/Men-Mars-Women-Venus-Understanding/dp/0060574216/

[11] After doing your due diligence, if there is an opportunity for you to attend a Christian couples' retreat, I highly recommend it—irrespective of the number of years you have been married. It will be a blessing!

The world is getting polluted with perverse ideas on choice, abortion, sexuality, and gender identity. Yet we are called to take care of the poor: the orphans and widows. God cares about social justice. Immensely. He is also holy. *Infinitely* holy and so different from us. He wants us to avoid, resist, repent, and emulate His holiness.

God-Point.

1.7.   Burning Bush Recommendations

The first book of the Bible is Genesis. The last is Revelation. All the Burning Bushes captured in the different chapters of the book series could be found between Genesis and Revelation. Bible quotes within context is important. As we shall see, the composition, the message, and the very existence of the Word of God is a Burning Bush, and we shall dedicate a chapter to it.

We noted above Moses could have just walked by the strange and amazing sight. In Revelation 2:4 we read:

> I hold this against you: You have forsaken the love you had at first.

Also, in Revelation 3:16 we read:

> Because you are lukewarm—neither hot nor cold—I am about to spit you out of my mouth.

Both verses reflect a characteristic of two different churches. The commonality? Apathy! God wants us to be *passionate* about Him and the world around us. In Deuteronomy 6:5 (also repeated in the New Testament), we read:

> Love the Lord your God with all your heart and with all your soul and with all your strength.

The emphasis is on *all* and it is holistic. So, the Lord is for passion and against apathy. We cannot just ignore the Burning Bushes that are screaming for attention and go about our business. We cannot afford to.

We are living in very strange times. The strangeness is an aggregate of many Burning Bushes. We need to understand—but not be corrupted by—the spirit of this age. The Lord is relying on us to bring about His kingdom.

Dealing with Burning Bushes is not comfortable. Like Moses, we need to leave our routines, perhaps even subject our sheep to some vulnerability, and go and check the strange and amazing sight. *Then* God will speak. Not before. He is waiting for us.

So, what is the recommendation?

For this chapter, it is *your resolution*, wholehearted and passionate resolution to learn about the Burning Bushes and consider the recommendations at the end of each chapter. You will probably come up with others and better ones for your own context.

The following pages will have material here that might make you feel uncomfortable. Decide to hang in there and never lose your passion. It is easy to develop a comfortable "gated community" mentality. Resist it and pursue the Burning Bushes as much as you can. Ask for wisdom and understanding, and He will give it to you.

You have started on your journey navigating the Burning Bushes. Sometimes it might feel uncomfortable, but I assure you, it will be exciting, and it will be a blessing.

Let the journey begin.

2. Classical vs. Fringe Christianity

2.1. Introduction

Christian churches of all denominations tend to focus on topics that are considered "safe," "classical," or (for lack a better name) "traditional" in their particular denomination.[12]

Outside the safe zone of topics that most biblical churches prefer to cover, there are many other "fringe" themes that are extremely relevant to our walk with God, the end-times, and even the health and existence of the Church. Most churches will not touch these subjects. However, the parishioners and especially the younger generations are very much interested with these topics, and the world has been providing them with "answers" and "explanations" that are completely contrary to the biblical narrative.

When was the last time you heard a sermon on *angels*? Or even *prophecy*? I recently attended a prophecy conference where it was mentioned that while 27 percent of the Bible is about prophecy, only 3 percent of the sermons address it. When was the last time you heard a sermon on Genesis 6 expounding upon fallen angels coming to earth, having intercourse with earthly women, and creating a race of giants? How about UFOs (now they are also called Unidentified Areal Phenomena [UAPs] by the US government)? What about aliens? Crop circles? Cattle mutilations? Modern miracles? Witches? Visons and apparitions? Ghosts? Paranormal activities? Shape-shifters? Transhumanism? Megalithic structures? Atlantis?

---

[12] Another term that gets associated with biblical Christianity—especially in the United States—is "*Conservative*" – in addition to "*Fundamentalist*." Liberal or progressive churches tackle topics that deal with issues such as social justice and racial equality but avoid many of the fringe topics mentioned here. The Bible has a lot to say about the poor and social justice, and often the progressive denominations have been spot-on with their involvement in social justice issues. Unfortunately, often the left-leaning denominations cover LGTBQ+ trends under the "social justice" umbrella. Some conservative denominations expose this unbiblical stance, and they are also spot-on. Underlying these convictions, lifestyles, and denominational tensions, there is a profound God-Point Burning Bush that will be addressed in volumes 3 and 4.

The list goes on and on.

There are also recent scientific trends such as quantum physics (aka quantum mechanics) that are having profound ramifications on the understanding of ourselves and the universe.

Some of these topics are supernatural par excellence. Other topics, such as UFOs, are physical and engineered but involve superior technology that violate the known laws of physics (hence *super*natural or *extra*terrestrial in some sense). Sometimes they exhibit metaphysical characteristics, such as abductees going through closed windows. But the secular world would hear none of it. For instance, when it comes to UFOs, for a long time, professional pilots—including in the military—avoided reporting for fear of being ridiculed or, worse, losing their jobs. Sometimes they were ordered not to mention what they have witnessed.[13]

Equally amazing are megalithic earthly structures all around the globe with incredible astronomical and engineering technologies that defy natural explanations given the ancient (in most cases, preflood) age of these structures. The construction, size, and precision of these structures are nothing short of astounding. Who built them and why?

---

[13] Interestingly, that started to change in 2017 when the *New York Times* and subsequently national media, such as Fox News and CNN, started reporting that the United States has technology not of this world. We shall cover it in *Volume IV: Signs and Wonders—The End of Times*.

Professionals in the secular world avoid and ridicule non-traditional explanations of these fringe topics. For instance, archeologists have their own strong-held Darwinian opinions on the succession of civilizations. Discoveries that challenge their narratives are either suppressed or ridiculed. There are reports of skeletons of giants that are sent to the Smithsonian[14] only to be either lost or destroyed, conveniently disappearing since they challenge the religiously held narrative of Darwinian evolution. The author, researcher, and filmmaker L. A. Marzulli[15] is spot-on when he emphasizes repeatedly in his programs and presentations (which I had the privilege of attending many times): there is a hidden history that has been deliberately obfuscated from the peoples of the world.

Although the world avoids these topics or provides what it considers "natural" explanations—including mass hypnosis, delusion, and wild imaginations—Christians need to take a very close look at these Burning Bushes.

2.2.   Stagnation in Gated Communities

The state of Christendom with all its diversities could be explained through the analogy of a complex cosmopolitan city. The city has many neighborhoods and areas. It also has gated communities. Sometimes churches act as a gated community: in their doctrines, preferred topics, comfortable Bible passages, traditions, and worldviews.

They avoid or are apprehensive of "outsiders" and "outliers."

Many Christian congregations feel comfortable within their own circles, even specific Bible passages, theologies, nomenclature, and topics. They prefer not to venture out. There is even a level of comfort

---

[14] You will also find media stories claiming these stories of giants and Smithsonian destroying them is a hoax—the existence and evidence of giants is too compelling to ignore though. You be the judge, https://ancientpatriarchs.wordpress.com/2016/04/19/giants-not-allowed-by-smithsonian-institute-disappeared-from-history-as-reported-in-old-news/

[15] https://lamarzulli.net/

and protection reflected in specific demographics. Not blatant (at least most recently) but sometimes implicit racism raises its ugly head in these gated communities.

However, the city representing Christianity is much bigger than the gated community of specific congregations. There are many neighborhoods reflecting not only Christian communities or congregations with different traditions, perspectives, or worldviews but also topics that are outside the realm of the gated and protected communities.

The traditionalism, the safe topics, and the conventionally established, even what are called evangelical churches, take on many forms. I have been involved in Armenian Evangelical churches for a couple of decades. While there have been moments of spiritual activities and growth, overall, the structure and direction of the Armenian Evangelical movement—like most evangelical churches in the West—has become ossified. The word I use reluctantly is *dead*.[16]

Churches are dying. The Pew Research Center recently found that the percentage of American adults who identified as

---

[16] https://www.faithward.org/why-are-churches-dying-and-what-can-you-do-about-it/

Christians dropped 12 percentage points in the last decade alone. So what happened? Why have so many people stopped looking to the church for guidance?

Our culture is changing more rapidly than it ever has before. And as the culture changes, so does what people need from church. But according to Fuller Theological Seminary professor Scott Cormode, the North American church hasn't kept up with people's changing needs.

Recently, at a conference I had attended, Dr. Michael Lake,[17] in a presentation titled "It Isn't Working: Time to Biblically Retool Church," shared some compelling and worrisome statistics:

- Four thousand new churches begin each year, and 7,000 churches close.
- Over 1,500 pastors left the ministry every month last year.
- Over 1,300 pastors were terminated by the local church each month, many without cause.
- Over 3,500 people a day left the church last year.
- Eighty percent believe pastoral ministry has negatively affected their families.
- Many pastors' children do not attend church now because of what the church has done to their parents.
- Sixty-six percent of church members expect a minister and family to live at a higher moral standard than themselves.

The currents and challenges to Christianity are many. Naturalism has been perhaps the most destructive trend. Dr. Francis Schaeffer,[18] who has had a tremendous impact on my spiritual growth through

---

[17] https://www.facebook.com/michael.k.lake/

[18] https://www.thegospelcoalition.org/article/know-your-evangelicals-francis-schaeffer

his books, indicated even in the twentieth century, "Our generation is overwhelmingly naturalistic." Naturalism has only what the secular world considers the "natural" as its source and reference point. Naturalism, at its core, removes God and His supernatural presence, deeds, Word, and presence completely out of reality and delegates it to myths and fairy tales—escapism for the weak, those who need a clutch to hang on, those who are "unscientific" and "irrational." As we shall see from the history of science and especially the latest trends in science and technology, the exact opposite is true. Honest scientists are discovering God! The evidence is overwhelming, and naturalism has failed on many fronts. Unfortunately, what is sometimes replacing it is not the return or rekindling of Christianity but rather a return to pagan worldviews and even to pagan gods. We will also expand upon this.

Going back to the state of churches, stagnation and naturalism have had devastating effects, causing sluggishness and death of churches. On the one hand, following the river of the cultural trends, many Christians lost their way. We should not underestimate the impact of theological seminaries that planted seeds of doubt and confusion into the minds of young seminarians without being intellectually or scientifically honest. The claim, of course—in the name of scholastic integrity—is the opposite. Some of these seminaries think and believe that *they* are the scholastically and intellectually superior with high standards of integrity. But having been in academia for decades, I have seen how "truth" can be made what the academicians want it to be—through downplaying or even misrepresenting the facts. Don't get me wrong. In secular or theological seminaries, there are many honest academicians. I have had the privilege to learn and interact with many of them. However, often what is happening in universities today is nothing less than dishonest, antiscientific voices trying to silence any different and descending view. It is sad but true!

When it comes to more—for lack of a better name— "conservative" Christianity, the diminishing of the supernatural manifests itself in several ways:

- *Carnal Christianity:* Let me elaborate through an example. I have been in church council meetings where the meeting starts through a prayer "we ask these in the name of our Lord Jesus Christ." Then the meeting continuous as if Christ is asked to leave the room and now the participants behave and interact exactly as they would in secular boards. Then at the end, Jesus Christ is invited back to the meeting for the closing prayer. This is how naturalism manifests itself in church councils. There are many facets to this carnality— including how the pastors are often treated as hirelings and how the church is run by few families who hold the reins of power and control: much the same way private organizations are run. There are many other facets of carnality infiltrating Christianity—especially through materialism.

- *Cessationism Christianity.* This idea permeates many traditional congregations. The idea is that the gifts of the Holy Spirit—such as miracles, speaking in tongues, prophecy, and healing as listed in 1 Corinthians 12—have ceased and are no longer applicable in the post-apostolic age. Now you will find many believers in these traditional congregations who believe in miracles, etc. But the Church does not seek them in its bylaws or practices. She (the Church) cannot identify those who have supernatural gifts. In a biblical church, 1 Corinthians 12 and other biblical passages, such as Ephesians 4:11-16, should be encouraged. The Church should continuously grow to maturity, leveraging the gifts of the Holy Spirit so that all believers can manifest the fruit of the Holy Spirit.

- *Comfortable Christianity.* The third category is much more pervasive. I often give the analogy of a city. If you think of Christianity (or Christian topics, to be precise), there are gated communities where we are very comfortable in, and we do not want or even dare to venture outside our circle of comforts. If you check most of the sermons that now are posted in abundance via social channels, you soon realize the commonality of the "safe" topics and the avoidance of certain passages or even events happening around us— such as Unidentified Flying Objects—with tremendous implications but little deep biblical understanding. These are taboo and "fringe" neighborhood topics.

There are many topics "outside the gate" or the comfort zone of most Christian congregations. Furthermore, most pastors are not equipped to deal with them. There are controversial topics that traditional churches won't touch. Of course, one argument is, how do such topics edify the Church or lead sinners to Christ? Shouldn't the Church or pastors just preach the Word?

Christianity is very much a struggle—a wrestle, a battle. According to Ephesians 6:12:

> For our struggle is not against flesh and blood, but against the rulers, against the authorities, against the powers of this dark world and against the spiritual forces of evil in the heavenly realms.

It is going against the current trends of the world dominated by the prince of the power of the air representing Satan and his minions. We are in a real spiritual battle, and we can see its impact all around us.

The Church as well as each one of us as a believer need to face the battle on all fronts: the enemy will always attack in our weakest fronts. We cannot afford it.

2.3.   The Battle of Many Fronts

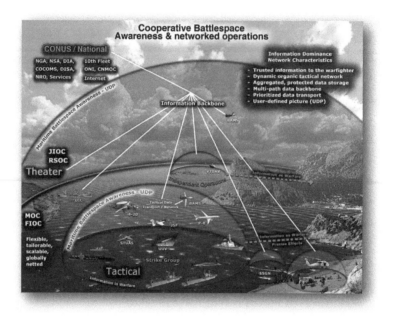

Throughout my career, I have had opportunities to research the application of digital technologies and especially Digital Transformation for military applications. I have visited the Pentagon as well as military contractors such as Lockheed Martin, Northrop Grumman, and Raytheon to present, discuss, and recommend various operational optimization as well as digital automation solutions for wasteful and inefficient operations in the military. In one of these ventures, I collaborated in a research on battlefields. This illustration comes from a paper titled "IoT with iBPM & DCM for Battlefield Digital Transformation."[19] An essential premise is that process-oriented collaboration between all units and all fronts is needed to win battles. We need to be prepared, collaborative, and vigilant on all fronts. Complex battles involve many units, armies, strategies, and tactics. If a battle is a value chain, that chain is as strong as the weekest link!

---

[19] It is a chapter in the book *Digital Transformation with Business Process Management*, https://bpm-books. com/products/digital-transformation-with-bpm-digital-edition My co-author was at that time working for Raytheon.

The fronts are many. Christians cannot afford to focus on "safe" topics and familiar approaches and expect to make an impact on the world. The enemy is smart and, in many ways, is winning on several fronts that have been left unprotected and vulnerable. Thank God, there are solid Christ-centered soldiers of the Lord who are fighting on those fronts that traditional Christianity would not touch.

The world is changing at an alarming rate. Information—not necessarily knowledge or wisdom—is exploding, doubling every six months or so.

These topics—such as angels (fallen or otherwise), UFOs and giants—are interrelated. They provide a very real supernatural perspective of the world around us. More than that, they are core to the relationship between God and humanity. They are also core to the "seed war" between God and the serpent.

It is interesting to note that the US military is very much interested in UFOs because of potential security threats. As we shall see in a subsequent chapter, there are also claims that the US military is collaborating with "aliens."

The secular world is providing its own perverse perspectives, while Christians either avoid or starve for knowledge. The entertainment world is saturated with shows, movies, and literature on superheroes. When I was a young man, my favorite superhero was Superman. Well, he was an alien! Today we are inundated with superheroes of the DC and Marvel comic books (now movies) and have rich collection of superheroes to pick from. Some of these superheroes are ancient gods.

If Christians do not take the lead in explaining these many Burning Bushes, the secular world with its own anti-Christian message and worldview will. It has done so, for instance, through popular TV programs such as *Ancient Aliens*.[20] Worse, the Luciferian

---

[20] https://en.wikipedia.org/wiki/Ancient_Aliens

movements and "religions" will even twist the evil as good, which we know will end up culminating through the appearance of the Antichrist.

Another obvious one, especially post 2017, is the disclosure of UFOs, which are now called UAP (Unidentified Areal Phenomena). There are many others.

Christian churches of all genres, especially in the spectrum from liberal to conservative within the evangelical circles as well as Catholic and Orthodox denominations, by and large tend to focus on select core topics and stands while ignoring many of the fringe topics.

As an example, consider one of America's most popular megachurches: John MacArthur's Grace Church.[21] The doctrinal statement is very well done and lists all the core Calvinistic beliefs of the Church and its doctrinal topics. There is nothing wrong or unbiblical about the topics, even though I am not your run-of-the-mill Calvinist. That is not the point. But if you consider, say, their biblical quotes on angels, including fallen angels, you will notice the Genesis 6:1–2 passage and its profound implications on the state of humanity, the ultimate battle between good and evil, and the destiny of humanity is *not mentioned*:

> And it came to pass, when men began to multiply on the face of the earth, and daughters were born unto them, That the sons of God saw the daughters of men that they were fair; and they took them wives of all which they chose.

The term *sons of God* always refer to angels. These verses are unusual and strange. They imply union between angelic beings and human daughters. The resulting offspring were an abomination and an anomaly. The terms used in the Bible for the progeny of

---

[21] https://www.gracechurch.org/

this unholy union are *giants, Rephaim* and *Nephilim*. In Genesis 6:4 we read:

> There were giants in the earth in those days; and also after that, when the sons of God came in unto the daughters of men.

As we shall see in subsequent chapters, the Burning Bush of the corruption of the human gene pool was the main reason for the flood. We will cover many examples of "seed wars," even modern ones involving hybrids. So, this category of fallen angels who sinned and were imprisoned is not covered in the doctrinal statements of most denominations. We will expand upon these—giants and the Nephilim—in volume 4.

The prophet Enoch played a key, important, and unique role in this narrative. His work and the extrabiblical book allotted to him are another Burning Bush.

2.4.   The Book of Enoch

In Genesis 5:21–24, we learn about Enoch:

> And Enoch lived sixty and five years, and begat Methuselah: And Enoch walked with God after he begat Methuselah three hundred years, and begat sons and daughters: And all the days of Enoch were three hundred sixty and five years: And Enoch walked with God: and he was not; for God took him.

Enoch did not see death. God took him to His presence. There is only one other character in the Bible that we know of who also did not see death but was taken: Elijah.

In Jude 1:14–15, we read a quote that references Enoch:

> And Enoch also, the seventh from Adam, prophesied of these, saying, Behold, the Lord cometh with ten thousands

of his saints, To execute judgment upon all, and to convince all that are ungodly among them of all their ungodly deeds which they have ungodly committed, and of all their hard speeches which ungodly sinners have spoken against him.

This is a quote from the extrabiblical Book of Enoch. This book[22] accredited to this amazing prophet is ancient but not part of the Protestant or Catholic Old Testament canon. The book (also called the Book of the Watchers—the categorical name of the angels that fell) contains more detailed descriptions of the Genesis 6 narrative. The details of this insurgence as described in the Book of Enoch was very familiar to the Jewish scholars and the early Christians.

Dr. Michael Heiser, in his book *The Unseen Realm*,[23] explains the significance of the Genesis 6 incident and Enoch:

Genesis 6:1–4 is one of the most marginalized passages in the Bible. Many pastors and Bible students do all they can to avoid taking it at face value, opting for "safe" interpretations that allow it to be shelved. Second Temple Judaism gave it a prominent, almost central, role in understanding God's activity in history. This book seeks to demonstrate that it deserves that status. Genesis 6:1–4 is actually one of the most important, serving an important role in biblical theology. Consequently, discussing how it should be—and shouldn't be—interpreted is where we need to begin.

Every baptism is therefore a reiteration of the past and future doom of the Watchers in the wake of the gospel and the kingdom of God. Early Christians understood the typology of this passage and its link back to 1 Enoch and Genesis 6:1-4. This is why early baptismal formulas included a renunciation of Satan and his angels. Baptism was anything but routine. It was a symbol of spiritual warfare.

[22] Actually, there are three books—1 Enoch, 2 Enoch, and 3 Enoch—but the most popular of these is 1 Enoch, also called the Book of Watchers, https://en.wikipedia.org/wiki/Book_of_Enoch

[23] https://www.amazon.com/Unseen-Realm-Recovering-Supernatural-Worldview/dp/1577995562/

The Book of Enoch—and other books that are not found in the Protestant Bible (which consists of sixty-six books by forty authors)—provides further details to the Genesis 6 incursion.

Many seminaries teach what is called the Sethian interpretation of the *sons of God*—meaning they were humans who took wives for themselves from the women (Canaan's descendants). The Book of Enoch describes the same scenario in Enoch 6:

> And it came to pass when the children of men had multiplied that in those days were born unto them beautiful and comely daughters. And the angels, the children of the heaven, saw and lusted after them, and said to one another: "Come, let us choose us wives from among the children of men and beget us children."

So, it makes it very clear the watchers (the "sons of God" in Genesis 6) were fallen angels.

There is one very old denomination whose canon *does* contain the Book of Enoch. The Ethiopian Orthodox Tewahedo Church is one of the oldest in the world. It was established in 333. Like the Armenian Orthodox (aka Apostolic) denomination, the Ethiopian Orthodox church predates many Western churches.

The Ethiopian Orthodox Bible has several books that are not included in the canon of the sixty-six books of the Protestant Bible. One of these books is the Book of Enoch, the same book James quotes from.

We are mentioning the Ethiopian Orthodox not so much for its *emphasis* and extensive coverage of the Watchers, giants, and the Nephilim in its teachings and doctrine. You will be hard-pressed to find much coverage on this topic. We are just indicating that Enoch is considered part of the Ethiopian Orthodox Church's biblical canon and Enoch's coverage of the Watchers, the giants, and the Nephilim is one of the most extensive and reliable ancient texts.

It is also interesting to note that the Book of Enoch and its symbolism especially with reference to the fall of mankind and salvation is also covered by other Orthodox Christian sources, especially Jonathan Pageau.[24] He is notorious in symbolism and identifying *patterns* throughout scripture and human history. On Enoch he notes:[25]

> What's important is that also there's a sense in which now that these giants have bodies now these giants devour they eat they're hungry they eat the world they devour all which the labor of men produced until it became impossible to feed them and then they turned against men and they started to devour men.

> Now you can understand it in a narrative way as these giants have giant bodies that just eat and eat and eat, but you can also, of course, understand what it can also refer to in terms of civilizational manner; you can imagine these cities that devour through the desire of its elites that kind of gather, and it also devours men, of course.

---

[24] From his YouTube channel (https://www.youtube.com/@JonathanPageau/about): Jonathan Pageau is a French Canadian icon carver, public speaker, and YouTuber exploring the symbolic patterns that underlie our experience of the world, how these patterns emerge and come together, manifesting in religion, art, and popular culture. He's also the editor of the *Orthodox Arts Journal* and host of the Symbolic World blog and podcast.

[25] https://youtube.com/watch?v=QtmLCK1keFI&si=EnSIkalECMiOmarE

He goes on to say:

> The book of Enoch can help us on can help us see how the patterns that are described in Genesis are one of the ways and one of the keys to helping us understand how the different manifestations of our world are connected together: how the different ways things are breaking down are not separate from each other but the relationship between desire and power and the breakdown the fragmentation the relationship between hybrids and technology. All of this is directly described in genesis and then built upon in the book of Enoch. It can help us understand our situation *now*, and it can also help us understand the way out.

In other words, the Book of Enoch and its elaboration of the Genesis 6 incident helps us understand the spiritual battles that are going on in the world today.

2.5. Catholic Perspectives

Fringe and avant-garde topics sound strange when affiliated with the Catholic Church. The Church prides itself as the most ancient of Christian denominations. You can't get more traditional than the Catholics! Having said that, throughout the centuries and especially more recently, various Catholic scholars and Catholic orders and even popes have dealt with topics that are outside the realm or focus of traditional Christianity. They even sponsor discussions and conferences on extraterrestrials.[26] Given the persecution of scientists such as Galileo by the Catholic Church, they have come a long way!

A couple of years ago, I was surprised to know that the Vatican had an observatory on Mt. Graham. Vatican Advanced Technology Telescope (VATT). The books, interviews, and videos of *Skywatch TV's*[27]

CEO Dr. Thomas Horn are invaluable. For instance, *Exo-Vaticana*[28] by the late Chris Putnam and Dr. Thomas Horn provides a summary of their visit to Mt. Graham observatory, and their interaction is interesting. Here is how they describe their visit:

> While we were given complete and unrestricted opportunity to question how the devices are used and what distinctively sets each of the telescopes on Mt. Graham apart, we had not expected the ease with which the astronomers and technicians would also speak of UFOs! This was especially true when we walked up the gravel road from VATT to the LBT, where we spent most of the day with a systems engineer who not only took us to all seven levels of that mighty machine—pointing out the LUCIFER device (which he lovingly referred to as "Lucy" several times and elsewhere as "Lucifer") and what it is used for, as well as every other aspect of the telescope we tried to wrap our minds around. He also stunned us as we sat in the control room listening to him and the astronomers speak so casually of the redundancy with which UFOs are captured on screens darting through the heavens. Our friendly engineer didn't blink an eye, neither did any of the other scientists in the room, and we were shocked at this, how ordinary it seemed to be.

---

[28] https://www.amazon.com/-/es/Thomas-Horn/dp/0984825630

This book is highly recommended, and Dr. Horn continues to update and expand upon the role of the Vatican and how it relates to the destiny of the United States in some of his more recent books:

> The Jesuit father on duty that day (whom we got on film), who told us that among the most important research occurring with the site's Vatican astronomers is the search for extrasolar planets and advanced alien intelligence.

To make it even clearer what some in the Vatican leadership believe, Putnam And Horn provide their observations from one of the leaders, Father Josè Funes:

> When the L'Osservatore Romano newspaper (which only publishes what the Vatican approves) asked him what this meant, he replied: "How can we rule out that life may have developed elsewhere? Just as we consider earthly creatures as 'a brother,' and 'sister,' why should we not talk about an 'extraterrestrial brother'? It would still be part of creation," and believing in the existence of such is not contradictory to Catholic doctrine.

A more recent 2021 article[29] expounds the stands of many in the Catholic faith on UFOs, including some of the leaders in Catholic astronomy such as the head of the Vatican Observatory, Brother Guy Consolmagno (also mentioned by Horn in many of his publications). When asked if he would be willing to baptize an alien, he said "Only if she asked."

The implications are profound, and this is only the tip of the UFO as well as science and faith positions in the Catholic Church. Now being a large, historic, and complex organization, there are many views on ETs and other topics such as evolution and science in the Catholic community.

---

[29] https://www.americamagazine.org/faith/2021/05/19/ufo-alien-life-catholic-church-240702

I have since subscribed to the Vatican Observatory newsletter.[30] There are always interesting scientific topics that are covered. Here is how they described the observatory:

> Observatory is one of the oldest active astronomical observatories in the world, with its roots going back to 1582 and the Gregorian reform of the calendar.
>
> Headquartered at the papal summer residence in Castel Gandolfo, outside Rome, this official work of the Vatican City State supports a dozen priests and brothers (Jesuits and diocesan) from four continents who study the universe utilizing modern scientific methods.
>
> Other collaborators of the Observatory include adjunct scholars (clergy and lay men and women) from many scientific disciplines, and scientists at major astronomical institutions around the world.
>
> They stand at the forefront of scientific research covering a broad range of topics, from an examination of the tiniest specks of interplanetary dust to the origin and structure of the universe.

Among the resources referenced on the website, you can find an interesting book titled *Would You Baptize an Extraterrestrial?*[31] coauthored by Guy Consolmagno, the director of the Vatican Observatory.

2.6. "Fringe" Christianity

The topics above—from Protestant, Pentecostal, Charismatic, Evangelical, Orthodox, or Catholic sources—are not conventional or traditional topics that we hear in churches. They are unusual

---

[30] https://www.vaticanobservatory.org/

[31] https://www.amazon.com/Would-You-Baptize-Extraterrestrial-box/dp/0804136955

topics. I want to use the term *fringe* very carefully in the book series and elucidate the context. Here I *do not mean* denominations or movements that are considered near but not core Christian, such as Seventh-Day Adventists, Jehovah's Witnesses, Unification Church, or Mormons. Neither do I mean Christian movements or approaches that deal with social issues or causes.

Rather, by *fringe*, I mean those topics "outside the gate" or comfort zone of most Christians, including supernatural gifts and manifestations but also giants, UFOs, and other similar topics.

Within various denominations there is a spectrum of fringe Christianity. There are Bible-believing Christians who have come out of traditional denominations to tackle topics that most traditional pastors or congregations will not touch.

There is a spectrum of these organizations, and on some topics or areas, they intersect and cross-pollinate.

1. *Charismatic and Pentecostal: Supernatural Gifts of the Holy Spirit.* The Holy Spirit are listed in 1 Corinthians 12:8–10.

> To one there is given through the Spirit a message of wisdom, to another a message of knowledge by means of the same Spirit, to another faith by the same Spirit, to another gifts of healing by that one Spirit, to another miraculous powers, to another prophecy, to another distinguishing between spirits, to another speaking in different kinds of tongues, and to still another the interpretation of tongues.

So, the gifts are:

- wisdom,
- special knowledge,
- faith,
- healing,

- miracles,
- prophecy,
- distinguishing between spirits (discernment),
- tongues, and
- interpretation of tongues.

There are many Charismatic and Pentecostal denominations that believe in the operation of these gifts in the Church today. Therefore, if we consider Charismatic and Pentecostal mainstream, then the operation of the supernatural gifts of the Holy Spirit is not fringe.

Most traditional Christian denominations do not believe these gifts are operational today. They are essentially *Cessationists*—meaning these gifts have stopped operating primarily after the completion of the biblical canons. One notable example of a Cessationist is John MacArthur:[32]

> The very claim in question is whether the miraculous gifts have continued past that foundational apostolic era. To simply appeal to those texts, which were addressed to believers during a time in which the gifts were operational, and to assume Christians are to apply and obey them in precisely the same way today.

In his book *Strange Fire*,[33] he further expands on the "dangers" of the manifestations within the Charismatic and Pentecostal denominations—from his perspective.

2. *Fringe Christianity Organizations and Channels.* A spectrum of Christian organizations—solidly founded on the Word of God—

---

tackles topics that conventional denominations often avoid. These range from prophetic gifts to miracles, supernatural healings, and much more.

One of the most recognized leaders in the field of the supernatural is Sid Roth.[34] He hosts the *It's Supernatural!* Television show and interviews a whole spectrum of guests with often unusual supernatural gifts and manifestations.

There are many others that deal with prophecy, end of times, and fringe topics such as UFOs, giants, secret societies, conspiracies, quantum mechanics, end-time prophecies, the multiverse, to name a few. Here are some of them:

- *Skywatch TV*, https://www.skywatchtv.com/
- *The Daily Renegade*, https://www.dailyrenegade.com/
- *Koinonia House*, https://www.khouse.org/
- *L A Marzulli*, https://lamarzulli.net/
- *Prophecy Watchers*, https://prophecywatchers.com/
- *Gen 6 giants—Steve Quayle*, https://www.gen6giants.com/
- *Douglas Hamp*, https://www.douglashamp.com/
- *Timothy Alberino*, https://timothyalberino.com/
- *Dr. Michael Heiser, https://drmsh.com/*
- *Time to Believe, https://www.timetobelieve.com/*
- *The Fringe, https://www.but-thatsjustme.com/the-fringe/*

This list is not exhaustive. Please follow the QR code at the end of this chapter to get these and additional links that will be added periodically. We shall dedicate a chapter for many (impossible to do all) of the topics covered by the "Fringe" Christianity topics.

---

[34] https://sidroth.org

2.7.   Recommendations and Takeaways

By and large, Christian denominations have focused on the core Christian traditions. I was born and raised an Armenian Apostolic (aka Orthodox) but have served in several evangelical churches, including Free Evangelical and Armenian Evangelical churches on the West Coast and East Coast of the United States. I have also been a member of the Church of God and attended several Catholic and Orthodox churches while living in Lebanon.

In *none* of these communities or their respective conferences have I ever heard any treatment or discussion of several of the fringe topics mentioned in this book series! I have since discovered passages in scripture dealing with some of these fringe topics that have never been covered in any sermon, and I have heard thousands of conventional sermons in the aforementioned churches and even preached several myself!

Protestants also have mainline denominations that tend to be liberal as well as more conservative Evangelical and Christ-centered Charismatic and Pentecostal churches. Evangelical churches tend to be more conservative and sometimes are labeled as "fundamentalist"—a horrible and prejudiced depiction. So, there are many ways to slice the Christendom pie: Liberal, Conservative, Fundamentalist, Evangelical, Charismatic, Pentecostal, Catholic, Orthodox, and others. There are several denominations within these groups: for instance, mainline Protestant churches can be Methodists, Episcopalians, and Southern Baptists. The Apostles' Creed and the Nicene Creed are early examples of core beliefs shared by traditional Catholic, Protestant, and Orthodox churches.[35] There are many—too many—Christian denominations, and we will also dedicate a chapter in volume 3 to this sad reality. It is not a good witness. There are social and "justice" issues such as gay marriage or ordaining gay

---

[35] Most Eastern Orthodox churches do not accept the Apostles' Creed. Some Protestant denominations ignore the early creeds.

ministers and, more recently, woke-ism and transgender causes that have divided some denominations,[36] even though the teaching of scripture is very clear. We shall treat these as Burning Bushes in subsequent chapters and volumes. However, what is interesting is the "unity" in most denominations when it comes to several of the fringe topics: they avoid them!

It is a dismal mistake.

To be clear and summarize, fringe topics include especially the UFO/UAPs[37] and the evidence of giants and the Nephilim. Some areas, such as gifts of the Holy Spirit (not to be confused with Fruit of the Holy Spirit that all Bible and Christ-centered congregations accept as core) are accepted and practiced by Pentecostal and some charismatic churches. But many other "fringe" topics are typically not handled or addressed head-on. Other powerful Burning Bushes include New Age, Supernatural manifestations, One World Government trends, revivals, and even the state of Israel, prophecy, and the return of our Lord Jesus Christ.

So, what are the recommendations?

- *Fear not.* The Word of God constantly encourages us not to be afraid. We need to be established in the Word and have a holistic view of all the topics. The battlefield has many fronts; we need to be vigilant. The enemy *is* a roaring lion, but we worship the Lion of Judah who has already won the battle! We need to have a bold, fearless, and holistic battlefield mentality and disposition.

- *Learn and apply.* We need to pursue, read, pray, and have fellowship as well as honest discussions on these

---

[36] Some churches and organizations have steered away so much that it is becoming difficult to recognize them as "Christian"—more on that in subsequent chapters. Some have even "succeeded."

[37] Unidentified Areal Phenomena are a more recent denotation by especially the US government, to distance the research, disclosures, and discussions away for UFO (Unidentified Flying Objects)—to preempt ridicule. Frankly, it's one and the same, but you will run in the "phenomenon."

topics. Most sermons—now on YouTube and other digital channels—tend to focus on "gated" similar topics. Don't get me wrong. There are some wonderful sermons and teachers of the Word out there, and they are a blessing. However, there are few and far between teachers of the fringe topics for a holistic perspective.

- *Become relevant.* Ultimately, our objective is to lead others to Christ. But we need to know where they are, what interests them, and what are they influenced by and then accordingly present the gospel. The fringe topics *do* have a following among the population at large, especially the younger generation. Churches are operating with "gated communities" mentality. We need to think outside the box through a deep understanding of the world around us while not being corrupted by it.

The following chapters (in volume 1 as well as volumes 2, 3, and 4) will be delving deep into topics that might sound strange or unfamiliar to some of you. The book will attempt to get you out of your gated environment and take you to some unfamiliar neighborhoods. It will try to equip you defensively and offensively for the spiritual battlefield. Even familiar topics such as the next two chapters on Jesus Christ and the Word could have themes that might sound strange. Stay on the course: fear not, learn, and become relevant—for your victories and witnesses.

3. The Burning Bush of Jesus Christ

3.1. Introduction

If you want to attack and destroy a movement, discredit its founder. No other movement or religion comes even close to the impact of Christianity—named after its founder, Jesus Christ.

From the accusation by the Pharisees that Jesus was casting out demons by Beelzebub (Matthew 12:24) to a caricature of the true Christ in Gnostic "gospels" to numerous erroneous depictions in different religions throughout the ages to modern-day attacks, no other person in history has been subjected to such erroneous semi-truths to outright vicious lies—to discredit Him in every way possible.

Our Lord Jesus Christ is also the *Word*, so it is not surprising to see the attacks on Him and the Bible often go hand in hand. We shall touch upon Jesus Christ in this chapter but have dedicated the next chapter to the Burning Bush of the Word of God; yes, if you want to destroy a movement, also discredit its Holy Book.

The true *historical* Jesus Christ[38] and the Word of God with its sixty-six books of canon containing the Old and New Testaments[39] have stood and withstood the test of time. That alone is an incredible Burning Bush.

---

[38] https://www.armenianorthodoxtheology.com/post/iconography-in-the-armenian-church

[39] *Canon* means the books that are included in scripture—the Holy Bible. Literally from Greek, it means "measure"—implying a book is included if it measures up to the standards of being included in scripture.

The entire history of mankind is divided between the period designated as Before Christ (BC) and the period after Christ: Anno Domini[40] (AD). This book is published in AD 2023. Now, more recently—due primarily to secular pressures—the preferred designation is Before Common Era (BCE), which is the same as BC, and Common Era (CE), which is the same as AD. Even though secular or non-Christian sensitivities have attempted to downplay Him, the fact remains our Lord Jesus Christ is *the* center of history.

Jesus is the only one in history who is fully divine and fully human. He is therefore the only one who can bridge the enormous gap between humanity and God.

The following sections describe *some* of the caricature and heretic views of our Lord Jesus Christ throughout the centuries.

3.2.   Jesus Is Made Up and Has Never Existed

The quest of the historic Jesus is an endless pursuit. There has been considerable efforts to disqualify the very existence of Jesus. A prime example of this is the well-known atheist Dan Barker:[41]

> The Jesus story is a combination of myth and legend, mixed with a little bit of real history unrelated to Jesus. Here's what I found out: 1) There is no external historical confirmation for the New Testament stories. 2) The New Testament stories are internally contradictory. 3) There are natural explanations for the origin of the Jesus legend. 4) The miracle reports make the story unhistorical. The Jesus of history is not the Jesus of the New Testament.

Barker is not alone. There are several prominent atheists, philosophers, and even those who have studied religion that cast

---

[40] The Latin of "in the year of the Lord"—the *Lord* being our Lord Jesus Christ.

[41] https://img1.wsimg.com/blobby/go/736cfcdc-0eaa-4e84-8bf2-045785c8eebe/downloads/1csiq3tlu_62424. pdf?ver=1620262371103

doubt on the existence of Jesus. When I was seeking for the truth prior to accepting Christ, I loved Bertrand Russell's *History of Western Philosophy*.[42] Here is how he questions the existence of Christ, from his lecture "Why I Am Not a Christian":[43]

> Historically it is quite doubtful whether Christ ever existed at all, and if He did we do not know anything about Him, so that I am not concerned with the historical question, which is a very difficult one.

However, the scholarly and honest intellectuals—even the agnostics and atheists among them—do accept the existence of Jesus based on the undeniable historic facts. From *The Second Coming of the New Age: The Hidden Dangers of Alternative Spirituality in Contemporary America and Its Churches*:[44]

> Dr. Bart Ehrman is the James A. Gray Distinguished Professor of Religious Studies at the University of North Carolina. He is an atheist historian who said the following at a conference on the historical evidence for the existence of Jesus: This is not an issue for scholars of antiquity. There is no scholar in any college or university who teaches classics, ancient history, New Testament, early Christianity, who doubts that Jesus existed. He is abundantly attested in early sources. Early and independent sources indicate that Jesus certainly existed. Paul is an eyewitness to both Jesus' disciple Peter and the brother of Jesus. Like, I'm sorry. *Atheists have done themselves a disservice by jumping on the bandwagon of mysticism because it makes you look foolish to the outside world.* He goes on to say in an article, "Whether we like it or not, Jesus certainly existed." (Italics mine.)

---

[42] https://www.amazon.com/History-Western-Philosophy-Bertrand-Russell/dp/0671201581

[43] https://users.drew.edu/~jlenz/whynot.html

[44] https://www.amazon.com/Second-Coming-New-Age-Spirituality/dp/1948014114

So much for the doubters of *the* center of the history of mankind. In addition to the Christian sources, there are undeniable, scholastic evidence of the existence of Jesus from non-Christian sources. Here are few of them from Josh MacDowell's *Evidence that Demands a Verdict:*[45]

> *Cornelius Tacitus* was a Roman historian who lived in approximately between AD 56 and Robert Van Voorst says Tacitus "is generally considered the greatest Roman historian" and his Annals is his "finest work and generally acknowledged by modern historians as our best source of information about this period."

In reference to the AD 64 fire, Tacitus writes:

> Therefore, to squelch the rumor, Nero created scapegoats and subjected to the most refined tortures those whom the common people called "Christians," hated for their abominable crimes. Their name comes from Christ, who, during the reign of Tiberius, had been executed by the procurator Pontius Pilate. Suppressed for the moment, the deadly superstition broke out again, not only in Judea, the land which originated this evil, but also in the city of Rome, where all sorts of horrendous and shameful practices from every part of the world converge and are fervently cultivated.

Another reliable source is the Jewish scholar and historian Josephus.[46] Flavius Josephus was a Jewish politician, soldier, and historian who lived around AD 37–100. He is considered one of the most important historians of Jewish origin. From *Evidence that Demands a Verdict:*

> Antiquities of the Jews was written by Josephus to explain the Jewish people and their beliefs to Romans in an effort to

---

[45] https://www.amazon.com/Evidence-That-Demands-Verdict-Life-Changing/dp/1401676707

[46] https://en.wikipedia.org/wiki/Josephus

reduce anti-Jewish bigotry. His writing is so influential that "all discussions regarding the Pharisees, Sadducees, Essenes, and Qumran community must take Josephus into account."

In his book *Antiquities*,[47] Josephus notes:

> At this time there appeared Jesus, a wise man, if indeed one should call him a man. For he was a doer of startling deeds, a teacher of people who receive the truth with pleasure. And he gained a following both among many Jews and among many of Greek origin. He was the Messiah. And when Pilate, because of an accusation made by the leading men among us, condemned him to the cross, those who had loved him previously did not cease to do so. For he appeared to them on the third day, living again, just as the divine prophets had spoken of these and countless other wondrous things about him. And up until this very day the tribe of Christians, named after him, has not died out.

Of course, there are scholars who debate authenticity of these sources. We will always have doubters. There is little we can do for those who have already made up their minds and are unwilling to consider rational, historical, scholarly, and scientific evidence.

47 https://www.amazon.com/Antiquities-Jews-Josephus/dp/1494452804

Let me also add a different perspective. The history of the Armenian people is very much tied to its conversion to Christianity in AD 301. On December 3 of each year, the Armenian Apostolic (aka Orthodox) Church commemorates two saints, two of the disciples of Jesus:[48] Saints Thaddeus and Bartholomew. These apostles were the first evangelizers of Armenia and were martyred there, giving the Armenian Church its apostolic identity and earning them the title "First Enlighteners of Armenia."

Thaddeus came to Armenia about AD 43 to preach Christianity. He was martyred in southeastern Armenia. His tomb lies in the Armenian Monastery of St. Thaddeus (Iran), where a chapel was built in the third century. Bartholomew is believed to have arrived in Armenia about AD 66. He was martyred in Hadamakert, southeast of Lake Van.

Note the dates. It will take an enormous amount of "faith" to think an entire nation with a solid, verifiable history and evidence would be fooled by a hoax of a Savior who never existed with martyrs who died for a fictious leader—with not a shred of evidence that Jesus Christ did not exist!

I don't think so.

3.3.   Jesus Is Just a Man

In the early 1970s, there was a popular musical titled "Jesus Christ Superstar."[49] One of the characters, Mary Magdalene, had a song on Jesus as "just a man":

> I don't know how to take this,
>
> I don't see why he moves me.
>
> He's a man, he's just a man,
>
> And I've had so many men before

---

[48] https://armenianprelacy.org/2022/11/30/saints-thaddeus-and-bartholomew/

[49] https://en.wikipedia.org/wiki/Jesus_Christ_Superstar

In very many ways,

He's just one more.

Well, Jesus is the Son of Man, and He is fully human—at the same time fully God. That is why He is the only mediator between humanity and God.

Jesus's divinity and His dual nature has been a controversial issue for centuries—even since the very conception of Christianity. As Mark Clark puts it in his seminal work *The Problem of Jesus:*[50]

> On the secular front, this topic has long been explored in what has been called the "quest for the historical Jesus," which began with Hermann Samuel Reimarus (1694–1768), who suggested that Jesus should primarily be understood as a Jewish revolutionary who failed to achieve his goals. Reimarus was followed by David Strauss (1808–74), who argued that much of what we have in the Gospels likely isn't what Jesus actually taught (and, specifically, should not include miracles). And then in the twentieth century Albert Schweitzer (1875–1965) suggested that Jesus should be seen as an apocalyptic prophet who expected the imminent end of the world, warning of impending judgment and doom, which did not come. This was followed by the demythologization of Jesus by Rudolf Bultmann (1884–1976), seen as the century's most influential New Testament scholar, and then most recently, the infamous Jesus Seminar, which distinguished the "Jesus of history" from the "Christ of faith" and concluded that Jesus didn't say or do most of what we think he did (less than 20 percent).
>
> The issue for these thinkers has never been whether Jesus existed—there is no doubt in their minds that he did. Instead, their desire is to show him as a man rooted in history and not mythology. Most of them deny he was God or that he claimed to be God at all.

---

[50] https://www.amazon.com/Problem-Jesus-Answering-Skeptics-Challenges/dp/0310108306

The Word of God—Jesus is also *the Word*—is the most obvious place to find the factual and historic view. Those around Jesus did not doubt His humanity or existence. Some doubted Him being the divine Son of God. The evidence of His humanity was complemented with the evidence of His divinity. His supernatural miracles compelled some of His accusers to make Him to be demonic. When Jesus was challenged and mocked on the cross to save himself, the implication is that He was just a human and the fact that He is not saving Himself according to the doubters "proved" He was just a human—not even a prophet with supernatural powers. Of course, His prophesized resurrection and victory over death proved them all wrong. The Jesus in "Jesus Christ Superstar" is a relatively modern depiction of this "only human" Jesus perspective, which has been going on for millennia.

3.4.   Early Christian Views on Jesus

As noted above, His contemporaries—even *with* the incredible evidence of His miracles—doubted His divinity and considered Him to be either demonic or just human. It is not surprising to find out that there were many heresies pertaining to His divinity. Dr. Patrick Hornbeck II does an excellent job summarizing and making more palatable the top historic heresies in "Top 10 Heresies in the History of Christianity."[51] Here are some of them:

- *Arianism*—Arians have been called the "archetypal" Christian heretics; accusations of Arianism have been made in almost every century since the fourth. Taking its name from an Egyptian priest, Arius, this heresy holds that Jesus, while the son of God, is neither eternal nor as fully divine as God the Father.

- *Docetists* proposed that the Son of God never fully took on human flesh and that the body of Jesus was an illusion,

---

just as Zeus in Greek mythology took the form of a bull to seduce Europa. Jesus, therefore, never physically died on the cross.

- *Nestorians*, another group of early Christians, believed that the human and divine persons of Jesus remained separate; thus, for them, "Jesus Christ" and "the Son of God" are not quite one and the same. Nestorian churches remained active in Persia and China as late as the eighth century.

The first Christian council of Nicaea convened to precisely address the heresy of Arianism.[52]

It is not surprising to find these different and even controversial beliefs and heresies in the formative years of Christianity. In fact, the nuances of some of these beliefs persist even today. One of these heresies that is making a comeback in this postmodern world is Gnosticism, which we address in the next section and following chapters on the Word of God and New Age.

3.5.   The Gnostic Jesus

In the next chapter on the Burning Bush of the Word of God, we shall delve deeper into the Gnostic Gospels. The Gnostics:[53]

> Saw Jesus's teachings not primarily as ends in themselves, but rather as means to another end: the inner mystical transformation they called "gnosis,"[54] the root of the word "Gnostic." The whole purpose of Christ's coming to earth had been to impart gnosis to people by awakening them to their true, divine nature, which had been covered over by the material world and forgotten. In support of these views, they could point to passages such as Luke 17:20–21 *Now*

---

[52] https://www.britannica.com/event/First-Council-of-Nicaea-325

[53] https://gnosticismexplained.org/jesus-christ-in-gnosticism/

[54] https://gnosticismexplained.org/gnosis/

when He was asked by the Pharisees when the kingdom of God would come, He answered them and said, "The kingdom of God does not come with observation; nor will they say, 'See here!' or 'See there!' For indeed, the kingdom of God is within you."

To understand the implications and ministry of the Gnostic Jesus, we need to appreciate the contrast the Gnostics put between the good god and the evil god. The latter in a much-perverted way corresponds to the God of the Bible! More specifically, the "good god" above is decoupled from the material world. The "evil god" created the world and is holding it captive. The Gnostics have the knowledge and secrets to "ascend" to the "good god."

How about Jesus? According to scholar Craig E. Evans:[55]

They wanted to take Jesus and make him part of this program and so they interpreted Jesus like a spy or a secret agent who descends from the god of light above takes on a disguise and looks like an ordinary human and then fools the evil powers and fools the evil God and shows his followers his gnostic followers a way out of this bleak mess a way of salvation through knowledge the early church wisely sought from what it was a gross distortion with no credibility Jesus of course never taught these things. So these Gnostic writings were condemned and Gnosticism as a teaching was regard heresy and in time it faded away and disappeared.

The problem is that it did not fade away completely. It is making a comeback especially these days—and more particularly when it comes to the New Age movement. We have dedicated an entire chapter to New Age in volume 3, another Burning Bush that has been having a devastating impact on many.

---

[55] https://www.craigaevans.com Quote from: https://youtu.be/FCul_DB0zzw

Here is a robust quote from the theologian N. T. Wright:[56]

> N. T. Wright, a modern scholar, adds: "Gnosticism in one or other of its many forms has been making a huge comeback in our day. Sometimes this has been explicit, as for instance in the New Age movements and similar spiritualities that encourage people to discover who they really are. Just as often, though, Gnosticism of a different sort has been on offer within would-be mainstream traditional orthodoxy."

Wright is not alone. Under the guises of New Age, feminism, transgender ideology, and other postmodern guises, Gnostic worldviews are making a comeback with a vengeance. It is a return to heathenism in the twenty-first century.[57]

> One of the prime opponents of early Apostolic Christianity was Gnosticism—a radical belief system that mixed pagan ideas, Greek philosophy, mysticism and human reasoning with twisted explanations of Scripture. Although Gnosticism faded from view after the 2nd century, many of its subversive and heretical ideas were *absorbed* into mainstream Christianity. Even more remarkable is that numerous scholars acknowledge that Gnostic ideas are *alive and growing* inside Christian churches and seminaries today. New Testament Professor Peter Jones documents the "striking parallels between the ancient heresy of Gnosticism and the spirituality of New Age thinking and the post-modern worldview" (*Spirit Wars*, 1997, p. vii). The dangerously deceptive doctrines battled by Paul, Peter, John and other early Apostolic leaders are being *revived today* with a vengeance—yet the average person is largely unaware of the real source of ideas promoted under the guise of progressive Christianity!

---

[56] https://johnharmstrong.typepad.com/john_h_armstrong_/church_tradition/page/4

[57] https://www.tomorrowsworld.org/magazines/2000/july-august/a-different-gospel

It does not stop there. Some have read an extraterrestrial Jesus in the Gnostic writings!

3.6.   Jesus the Extraterrestrial

In *The UFO That Took Jesus*,[58] Adrienne Jeffery commenting on his interpretation on the Gospel of Thomas—considered by some as one of the Gnostic "gospels"—sees extraterrestrial technology in some of its passages:

> There is a verse in the gospel of Thomas which depicts the planetary home of Jesus and its likeness i.e. the Kingdom of Heaven. Jesus is asked what it is like and his response is: "For there are five trees in Paradise for you; they do not change, summer or winter, and their leaves do not fall. Whoever knows them will not taste death." Jesus is alluding to the paradise which is the place in which he came from. While prominent academics have argued that this saying is a reference to the tree of life in the garden of Eden (see Gen. 1–3), I would argue that these five trees are metaphorical symbols for some kind of innovation, medicine or knowledge which humanity at the time of the writing of the gospel of Thomas did not comprehend. This could be immortality, true knowledge or something similar. Whatever it is, it is unchanging and permanent.
>
> Jesus promises health and eternal life in the place he calls home. This is consistent with many testimonies of abductees who make the claim of advanced scientific knowledge.

He continues with his description of why Jesus did not allow Mary to touch Him after His resurrection:

> In my view, based on not only this source but the accounts of the gnostic gospels, Jesus was taken up into a craft and

---

[58] https://www.amazon.com/UFO-That-Took-Jesus-Christ/dp/B085KJ7218

in John's account, he was being lifted after his body was restored by the Ones who took him up. That's why he didn't want Mary to touch him as he was in the process of being sucked into the vehicle.

We will delve much deeper into UFOs and extraterrestrials in volume 4. In the Christian context, the discussion has been more along the lines of the challenge of a UFO phenomenon to the Christian faith. Among evangelicals, it has remained mostly a fringe topic—as alluded to in chapter 2. However, as we noted, the Catholic Church has had serious discussions, conferences, positions, and even an observatory dealing with the UFO and the possibility of alien life. We also listed several robust Christ-centered evangelical organizations or thought leaders that are addressing this important fringe topic— often in the context of biblical prophecy.

There has been some discussion from UFO circles on the supernatural appearances in the Bible characterized as extraterrestrial. Erich von Däniken, the author of *Chariots of the Gods?*,[59] for instance, suggests replacing *angels* with *extraterrestrials* in reading the Bible. Also replace appearances such as the *chariots of fire* with *Unidentified Flying Objects*—technology form alien visitors.

This UFO visiting earth, potentially creating humanity through panspermia premised perspective on Jesus, is captured in a fictitious novel titled *Jesus the Extraterrestrial Trilogy Volume 1*[60] by Leo Mark:

> The stories about Jesus, the way Mary became pregnant while still a virgin—of course it must have been by artificial insemination: hence the legend of the Virgin Mary. Jesus' powers were explained. It was clear that he belonged to a race which was mentally very advanced, with total control over his own mind and, thereby, able to perform the "miracles" which everyone talks about.

[59] https://www.amazon.com/Chariots-Gods-Erich-von-Daniken-ebook/dp/B07RWPNK4N/

[60] https://www.amazon.com/Jesus-Extraterrestrial-Trilogy-Vol-Origins-ebook/dp/B004XT6D7S

The subtitle of the book is *Novel Based on Historic Documents.* Not sure what history he is referring to, but the same type of "confidence" in our extraterrestrial origins is implicit in the long-running *Ancient Aliens* series.

In the aforementioned book *The UFO That Took Jesus: The Truth About Who Christ Was*, Adrienne Jaffery provides an interesting explanation on this theory:

> Jesus goes into further detail about the creation of the world in one of proceeding parables of Matthew 13. "He told them still another parable: 'The kingdom of heaven is like yeast that a woman took and mixed into about sixty pounds of flour until it worked all through the dough.'" Jesus spoke all these things to the crowd in parables; he did not say anything to them without using a parable. So was fulfilled what was spoken through the prophet:

> "I will open my mouth in parables, I will utter things hidden since the creation of the world" (Matt. 13:31–35). In this parable, Jesus compares his home planet to ingredients which are the basis for making dough. He uses the exact measurement of sixty pounds of flour. This is a deliberate quantity and cultural context is very important in understanding why this measurement is so precise.

> In using this image, he actually is making two statements about the likeness of his home: the social climate of his home planet and how the planet will be made known to human kind in the future.

He further adds:

> Both Däniken and Rael have claimed that our Creators would have found solutions to the problems we have on earth: notably in this case: sustainable development and world peace. Jesus is promising a home for those who are broken, hungry and poor. Something which he does on many

> occasions in the gospels (most evident in the sermon on the mount in Matt. 5–7). Secondly, Jesus makes a statement about how the Kingdom will be revealed to mankind. Notice how each parable uses a process which has a primary cause.
>
> This is either a farmer, a master, a cook, and in this parable, a baker. This cause generates a process which produces visible produce through hard work. Jesus is making the claim that his Kingdom will be made known in the end. Just like a baker cannot see the beauty of a fully formed loaf in the initial baking process, we cannot visibly see the Kingdom or experience it in this world. We are the process. Our deeds are the ones which will save us or be our termination in the end. If we are to be saved, we will be able to profit from those loaves which will feed us in endless supplies.

The "Alien Jesus" narrative contains numerous contradictions at various levels. It has profound misunderstandings of the nature of God, the Trinity, and the very nature of Jesus taking on human form to save mankind. More on that in the following sections.

There are still other depictions of Jesus—far from the true Jesus. One of those that have influenced especially popular culture is the New Age Jesus.

3.7.   New Age Jesus

The New Age movement is one of the most pervasive trends that combines several pagan, mystical, and secular belief systems. Like many heresies and pagan religions, a core premise in New Age is that *we* are already "gods" or divine, and the New Age teachings and practices are to realize this godhood in us.

They have their own version of "Jesus." The very existence and influence of the New Age are a Burning Bush, and we shall go deeper into their belief in volume 3. Here the focus is on what they teach about Jesus. One of the best sources for understanding the

New Age is from New Agers themselves, especially those who were deep into it and, by the grace of God, discovered the true faith in our Lord Jesus Christ.

Steven Bancarz and Josh Peck are both believers in Christ who have come out of New Age; Steven used to be a leader in the movement. They have written an excellent book titled *The Second Coming of the New Age: The Hidden Dangers of Alternative Spirituality in Contemporary America and Its Churches*[61] that exposes the inconsistencies, heresies, and anti-Christian views in New Age. They elucidate what New Age teaches about Jesus Christ:

> In the New Age movement, lots of extravagant claims are made about Jesus of Nazareth, but none refer to the Jesus who existed in history. The attributes and properties given to the person of Jesus are so far removed from our historical records of Jesus that they cannot refer to Jesus. . . . Jesus is accused of believing in things that 100 percent of the historical records available tell us He full-on rejected.

> The attributes and properties given to the person of Jesus are so far removed from our historical records of Jesus that they cannot refer to Jesus . . . They are referring to an idea of Jesus that is diametrically opposed to everything we know about Him, a version of Him that has absolutely no record of having existed in the world . . . New Agers often justify their assertions about Jesus on the basis of private spiritual revelation and by isolating a small handful of words out of context.

> According to a theosophical foundation called Share International: The method he used is called spiritual overshadowing, that is, his consciousness informed and guided the actions and teachings of his disciple Jesus . . . The seemingly paradoxical claim that Jesus and the Christ are not

---

[61] https://www.amazon.com/Second-Coming-New-Age-Spirituality/dp/1948014114

the same person, in the literal sense of the word, is more reasonable than it would appear.

So, Jesus was only able to do what He did because of Lord Matraiya operating through Him. Matriaya came over Him in His baptism and was with Him until resurrection, giving Him the means by which to carry out the life He lived. Jesus is not unique, however, as Matraiya has also overshadowed Hercules, Hermes, Rama, Mithra, Vyasa, Confucius, Zoroaster, Krishna, Shankaracharya, Gautama, and Mohammed.

Some New Agers even challenge the existence of the historical Jesus and consider Him a mythological figure. One of the main lessons here is that when various heresies or movements use the term *Jesus Christ*, they might mean something entirely different from the Jesus Christ of the holy scriptures.

3.8.   Jesus in Islam

It might be surprising to most Christians—even scholars—and also Muslims that the Bible and the Quran agree on many of the attributes of Jesus:

- *Jesus is born of a virgin*. From Mariam (he is always identified as son of Mariam, which is unusual and implies born of a woman without a man):

    When the angels said, "Mariam, Allah gives you good news of a word from him, whose name will be the Messiah, Isa son of Mariam, highly exalted in this world and the hereafter, and brought near [to Allah]. (Aal Imran 3:45)

- *Jesus is sinless*.

    He said, "I am truly a messenger of your Lord to give you a sinless boy." (Mariam 19:19)

- *Jesus is the Word of God and Spirit from Him.*

> Truly the Messiah, Isa son of Mariam is Allah's messenger
> and his word which he sent down on Mariam, and a spirit
> from him. (Al-Nisa 4:171)

It is very interesting that of all the major religions, Islam, and specifically the Quran, is closest in its identification of the attributes of our Lord Jesus Christ.

While in Lebanon and attending the American University of Beirut, I was privileged to know and work as a servant of the Lord under the tutelage and leadership of Rev. Fouad Accad, who had authored "The 7 Muslim-Christian Principles (7MCPs)."[62] This was a focused (ministering to the Muslims, leading them to Christ within their cultural context) ministry spearheaded by The Navigators of the Middle East. I have used this incredible work that is based on thirty years of scholastic research by Rev. Accad and saw many Muslims come to Christ while quoting verses from the Quran (and of course, the corresponding verses from the Bible) as a bridge to Christ! The

---

[62] https://www.amazon.com/Fouad-Accads-Building-Bridges-3rd-ebook/dp/B0BS5LSJZJ/

picture is from one of the retreats. The beautiful lady on the lower left of the picture is Silva. She became my wife and soulmate for forty years. I am the hairy dude on the upper right. This book is dedicated to Silva!

Building Bridges is an excellent book and a must-read for all Christians to better understand Muslims, what they believe about Christ, and how we can build bridges. It contains the 7 MCPs with descriptions. Rev. Accad gives many examples from his own life. He is also an excellent scholar and gives several examples of misconceptions that Muslims have about Christians and vice versa. His loving approach is building bridges, even using the Quran as a bridge to lead Muslims to Christ.

Rev. Accad's approach is based on a deep love, respect, understanding, and sensitivity to the Muslims. I was so impressed by his deep knowledge of the Quran, and I have seen the appreciation and respect of the Muslims when they interacted with him and were surprised by his deep knowledge. His approach is biblical. It is based on Paul's Acts 17 example. From *Building Bridges:*

> When Paul was in Athens, he met with fellow Jews on their own turf, which was their synagogue. He did not tell them to change their day of worship, but instead went to their place of worship on their special day. By working among them within their religious, cultural, and national life, he built a bridge for the good news. We must follow this example. Western Christians have traditionally rejected the cultural and religious customs of Middle Eastern Muslims, thinking that Western cultural and religious traditions are superior. Muslims have often rejected much of Western culture, which they see as immoral and opposed to traditional values. They both typically suggest that others adopt their culture. They think that only those who follow their culture and customs are members of God's people. As we build bridges, we must seek to understand and adapt to each other.

For each of the Seven Muslim-Christian principles, Rev. Accad, who had a very deep understanding of the Quran as well as the Bible, quotes from the Christian and Islamic scriptures for each principle. Ultimately, the reader is led to faith in Christ. For instance, the following is the sixth principle on accepting Christ. Please notice the terminology and approach. *Isa* is the Arabic and Quranic name for Jesus.

> *Principle 6: Making Him Ours*
>
> The word "Islam" means submission to Allah's will, or turning our face toward Allah and accepting his will and his plan of salvation for our lives. This involves fearing Allah and accepting the ransom and mercy he has offered us through Isa, his word.
>
> We can be saved not by Allah's mercy in general but specifically through Isa, who is the word of Allah and mercy from Allah. We are saved when we repent, trust in Isa, and invite him to come into our lives as our master. Here are some passages that help explain this concept.

Then he follows it with verses from scripture for repentance and acceptance of Christ. Here is the sinner's prayer:

> I repent and turn to You now because I know that You love me and have provided a ransom for me. I trust in Isa, Your word, who took the punishment for my sins when he sacrificed himself as a ransom for me, and then was resurrected from the grave. I now surrender myself to You because of Isa, and I ask You to give me eternal life, peace, and a new heart that will honor You and reject sin. I repent from my sins and commit myself to follow and obey Al-Masih Isa. Thank You for hearing me. Amen.

Since the principles quote from the books acceptable to the Muslim, the approach here is not to make the culturally Muslim into a Western or cultural Christian. Instead, the goal is to lead them to Christ without alienating them. It is like the approach Paul used with the Athenians in Acts 17—where he explained who the unknown God was. I encourage you to read this book and see the many examples of how Muslims were converted, through building bridges, using their own scriptures and beliefs to lead them to Christ, that resulted in joy and changed lives (to say nothing of the eternity they gained through the Savior).

Rev. Accad also explains the very difficult questions or issues that have unnecessarily divided Christians and Muslims, such as Jesus being the Son of God or the Trinity. He always uses the scriptural sources as well-rational, compelling, and logical arguments to make the case of the common beliefs leading to Christ. For instance, what Muslims object to—God having a sexual relation to conceive a Son—is also what Christians reject. We agree He came through the Holy Spirit! Also, Christians believe in one God,[63] not three "gods," which, in the Muslim tradition, includes Mary as one of the "gods"!

3.9.   The Jesus Seminar

Before delving into the rather academic "Jesus Seminar" that attempts to pursue a quest for the historic Jesus, let me provide a brief background. I have four college degrees and have spent about a decade in universities. I have a BSc and an MSc in Mathematics as well as an MSc and PhD in Computer Science. I have also been a full-time and adjunct professor for many years. In case you missed my bio, I have also written hundreds of articles—many of them peer-reviewed—in various academic and business journals and authored ten books in Computer Science. My purpose is not to beat my own

---

[63] Of course, in three persons—but one God nevertheless—as mentioned and repeated so many times in scripture. Here is how Jesus described the most important commandment in Mark 12:29: "The most important one," answered Jesus, "is this: 'Hear, O Israel: The Lord our God, the Lord is one.'"

drum but rather provide the background for my academic and scientific research approach. I am and always have been a student of science and pure research. I just love it!

I also appreciate pure, unadulterated, and honest research and academics. I admire honest scholarly research by specialists who attempt to discover the truth. Having said that, I have seen my share of less-than-honest and slanted research in even the most recent and advanced of the sciences—Computer Science.[64] I can tell stories from research that could surprise you. Sometimes the behavior of professors and scientists are not that different from what you find in politics or business. It is sad but true. But please remember, scientists are humans who are also tempted by vanities.

Unadulterated objectivity—even in science—goes so far. We each have our biases, frailties and our own eyeglasses through which we view the world. It even happened with Einstein. Personal bias is bad enough in science. Unfortunately, it is much worse in the humanities. We are dealing with opinions and conjecture. There are always prejudices for subject matters have serious ramifications on our own personal lives and choices. Jesus Christ is one—if not the most important—of these topics.

The Jesus Seminar is an interesting, serious, yet slanted reactionary view that is, unfortunately, less than honest or factual. The effort on such an important topic is commended. The approach as well as the "scholars" are slanted to one side—the so-called liberal[65] one—and the conclusions are misleading, to say the least.

---

[64] Computer Science is often misunderstood and not treated as seriously as the other traditional sciences. Do not be surprised if you tell someone you are a Computer Science major and they will ask you if you can fix their printer! To be clear, I have had my share of frustrations with printers and other devices. But fixing printers is not in the realm of Computer Science!

[65] I dislike the label *liberal* as much as I dislike *fundamentalist* and *conservative*. It has caused so much confusion and division. Usually in the United States, the Democratic Party is known for its liberal stands and the Republican Party for its conservative ones. Those of us who identify with positions on both platforms are left homeless and confused. I have stopped voting.

Here are some of their conclusions from their website:[66]

- Jesus of Nazareth did not refer to Himself as the Messiah, nor did He claim to be a divine being who descended to earth from heaven in order to die as a sacrifice for the sins of the world. These are claims that some people in the early church made about Jesus, not claims He made about Himself.

- At the heart of Jesus's teaching and actions was a vision of a life under the reign of God (or in the empire of God) in which God's generosity and goodness are regarded as the model and measure of human life; everyone is accepted as a child of God and thus liberated both from the ethnocentric confines of traditional Judaism and from the secularizing servitude and meagerness of their lives under the rule of the empire of Rome.

- Jesus did not hold an apocalyptic view of the reign (or kingdom) of God—that by direct intervention, God was about to bring history to an end and bring a new, perfect order of life into being. Rather, in Jesus's teaching, the reign of God is a vision of what life in this world could be, by being a miraculous act of God.

It is also good to quote the overall context and background convictions of the "researchers" who came up with this conclusion. Let me give an example from the book titled *The Five Gospels*,[67] a publication of the seminar:

> The Five Gospels represents a dramatic exit from windowless studies and the beginning of a new venture for gospel scholarship. Leading scholars—Fellows of the Jesus Seminar—have decided to update and then make the legacy

---

[66] https://www.westarinstitute.org/seminars/jesus-seminar-phase-1-sayings-of-jesus

[67] https://www.amazon.com/Five-Gospels-Really-Search-Authentic/dp/006063040X

of two hundred years of research and debate a matter of public record.

In the aftermath of the controversy over Darwin's The Origin of Species (published in 1859) and the ensuing Scopes "monkey" trial in 1925, American biblical scholarship retreated into the closet. The fundamentalist mentality generated a climate of inquisition that made honest scholarly judgments dangerous. Numerous biblical scholars were subjected to heresy trials and suffered the loss of academic posts. They learned it was safer to keep their critical judgments private. However, the intellectual ferment of the century soon reasserted itself in colleges, universities, and seminaries. By the end of World War II, critical scholars again quietly dominated the academic scene from one end of the continent to the other. Critical biblical scholarship was supported, of course, by other university disciplines which wanted to ensure that dogmatic considerations not be permitted to intrude into scientific and historical research. The fundamentalists were forced, as a consequence, to found their own Bible colleges and seminaries in order to propagate their point of view. In launching new institutions, the fundamentalists even refused accommodation with the older, established church-related schools that dotted the land.

For those of us who are Christian and come from a scientific and scholarly backgrounds, these conclusions are intellectually untenable. They are also intellectually and historically dishonest.

Lee Strobel, in his seminal work *The Case for the Real Jesus*,[68] clearly articulates the challenge of the Jesus Seminar:

> For many people, their first exposure to a different Jesus came with extensive news coverage of the Jesus Seminar, a group of highly skeptical professors who captivated the media's attention in the 1990s by using colored beads to vote on what

---

[68] htttps://www.amazon.com/Case-Real-Jesus-Journalist-Investigates/dp/031024210X

Jesus really said. The group's conclusion: fewer than one in five sayings attributed to Jesus in the Gospels actually came from him. In the Lord's Prayer, the Seminar was confident only of the words "Our Father." There were similar results when the participants considered which deeds of Jesus were authentic. What made the Jesus Seminar unique was that it bypassed the usual academic channels and instead enthusiastically took its findings directly to the public.

"These scholars have suddenly become concerned—to the point of being almost evangelistic—with shaping public opinion about Jesus with their research," said one New Testament expert.[9] They found a ready audience in many Americans who were receptive to a new Jesus. With the public's appetite whetted, publishers began pumping out scores of popular books touting various revisionist theories about the "real" Christ. At the same time, the Internet spawned a proliferation of websites and blogs that offer out-of-the-box speculation about the Nazarene. An equal-opportunity phenomenon, the World Wide Web doesn't discriminate between sober-minded scholars and delusional crackpots, leaving visitors without a reliable filter to determine what's trustworthy and what's not. Meanwhile, college classrooms, increasingly dominated by liberal faculty members who grew up in the religiously suspicious 1960s, provided a fertile field for avant-garde beliefs about Jesus and Christianity. According to a landmark 2006 study by professors from Harvard and George Mason universities, the percentage of atheists and agnostics teaching at U.S. colleges is three times greater than in the population as a whole. More than half of college professors believe the Bible is "an ancient book of fables, legends, history, and moral precepts," compared to less than one-fifth of the general population.

Another source that challenges the findings and conclusion of the Jesus Seminar is captured in *Reinventing Jesus: How Contemporary*

Skeptics Miss the Real Jesus and Mislead Popular Culture.[69] It is interesting and telling how they characterize the Jesus Seminar and *The Da Vinci Code*:

> The seeds of radical skepticism have been widely sown by mass media for over a decade. From the Jesus Seminar—a fringe group of scholars whose color-coded version of the Gospels repeatedly made headlines in the 1990s—to the recent blockbuster novel and now movie The Da Vinci Code, skeptics of all stripes have used the popular media to promote their demoted versions of Jesus.

The many rich topics in the book include the challenges to the unique and historic virgin birth of Jesus and His resurrection.

> This movement started in 1985 and claims to build its conclusions upon 200 years of research on Jesus. Here is how one of their co-founders Robert Funk characterized their objectives:[70] "We want to liberate Jesus. The only Jesus most people know is the mythic one. They don't want the real Jesus, they want the one they can worship. The cultic Jesus."

In fact, those who truly want to find the *real* Jesus should do so through a Middle Eastern context; after all, that is where He was born. It is interesting and telling that the pseudo-intellectual scholars of the Jesus Seminar do not include profound contextual understanding of Jesus. The next section elaborates on this.

3.10. Jesus through Middle Eastern Eyes

Writing this book series has been a blessing. I am humbled by the scholarly giants who have been my teachers, inspiration, and guide

---

[69] https://www.amazon.com/Reinventing-Jesus-J-Ed-Komoszewski/dp/082542982X

[70] https://www.westarinstitute.org/resources/the-fourth-r/milestones-in-the-quest-for-the-historical-jesus/

as I compile the amazing Burning Bushes that are calling us to God throughout the centuries, especially the twenty-first century. It would be remiss of me not to mention Dr. Kenneth Bailey among those giants.[71] He was an amazing Bible scholar who has spent most of his life in the Middle East. I had the privilege of meeting him and learning from him in Lebanon, where he thought (amazing how I have never forgotten) about the parallelism in scripture. Here is Dr. Bailey:

> Beyond the commentaries, ancient and modern, lie the versions. I am convinced that the Arabic Bible has the longest and most illustrious history of any language tradition. The ancient Christian traditions translated the New Testament into Latin, Coptic, Armenian and Syriac. But by the fifth century those translation efforts stopped. Arabic New Testaments have survived from perhaps the eighth and certainly the ninth century. They were translated from Syriac, Coptic and Greek, and continued to be refined and renewed up until modern times. Translation is always interpretation, and these versions preserve understandings of the text that were current in the churches that produced them. They are a gold mine for recovering Eastern exegesis of the Gospels. These essays not only focus on culture but also on rhetoric. The peoples of the Middle East, ancient and modern, have for millennia constructed poetry and some prose using parallelisms. Known to the West as "Hebrew parallelisms" they are used widely in the Old Testament. But, early in the Hebrew literary tradition, these parallelisms were put together into what I have chosen to call "prophetic homilies." The building blocks of these homilies are various combinations of the Hebrew parallelisms. Sometimes ideas are presented in pairs that form a straight-line sequence and appear on the page in an AA BB CC pattern. At other times, ideas are presented and then repeated backward in an A B

---

[71] https://en.wikipedia.org/wiki/Kenneth_E._Bailey

CC B A outline. These can be called "inverted parallelism" (they are also named "ring composition" and "chiasm").

I have attended Dr. Bailey's presentations and seminars exposing this parallelism, and it was truly an eye-opener in understanding the scripture. This is a simple example of the depth of the Middle Eastern perspective in understanding the real and historic Jesus: His life, His works, His words, His accomplishments.

Here is a high-level table of content of the different parts handled in the book *Jesus Through Middle Eastern Eyes*.[72] Each of the chapters of these parts provides the scholarly references, explanations, and exposition, especially through the contextual Middle Eastern (especially Jewish) perspective.

- Part 1: The Birth of Jesus
- Part 2: The Beatitudes
- Part 3: The Lord's Prayer
- Part 4: Dramatic Actions of Jesus
- Part 5: Jesus and Women
- Part 6: Parables of Jesus

This is an amazing book and a must-read for all those who are interested in knowing the real historic Jesus in the context of His culture, Jewish background, and the context of history. Furthermore, those who are close to the cultural perspectives will capture the essence of His work, His words, and His message—accurately and historically.

What is amazing about Dr. Bailey's incredible scholarly work is, he lived sixty years in the Middle East and studied the languages, the culture, and the context of the area where Jesus came from. But

---

[72] https://www.amazon.com/Jesus-Through-Middle-Eastern-Eyes-ebook/dp/B001I461LY/

perhaps equally and even more important are his deep analysis and knowledge of commentaries and scholarly work from Middle Eastern authors. This is critical. For instance, the four principles of historic research described in Miller's *The Jesus Seminar and Its Critics*[73] overlooks the Middle Eastern perspective and fails to recognize the essential role of cultural context, as well as the contributions of Middle Eastern authors, translators, and commentators throughout centuries.

Will all due respect to the PhDs and scholars of the Jesus Seminar, this is weak scholarship, to say the least!

3.11.   Jesus Recommendations

C. S. Lewis[74] is one of my favorite Christian authors. He has an excellent challenge for those who have and continue to discredit the divinity of our Lord:

> I am trying here to prevent anyone saying the really foolish thing that people often say about Him [that is, Christ]: "I'm ready to accept Jesus as a great moral teacher, but I don't accept His claim to be God." That is the one thing we must not say. A man who was merely a man and said the sort of things Jesus said would not be a great moral teacher. He would either be a lunatic—on a level with the man who says he is a poached egg—or else he would be the Devil of Hell. You must make your choice. Either this man was, and is, the Son of God: or else a madman or something worse. . . . You can shut Him up for a fool, you can spit at Him and kill Him as a demon; or you can fall at His feet and call Him Lord and God. But let us not come up with any patronizing nonsense about His being a great human teacher. He has not left that open to us. He did not intend to.

---

[73] https://www.amazon.com/Jesus-Seminar-Its-Critics/dp/094434478X

[74] https://www.kevinhalloran.net/c-s-lewis-quote-on-jesus-as-liar-lunatic-or-lord/

There is an elegance and simplicity yet profound depth in Jesus Christ. He is the second person of the Trinity. He dwells in us through the Holy Spirit, the third person of the Trinity. He represents us and constantly intercedes for us with the Father, the first person of the Trinity. The scripture has many *names* for Christ. Each name represents an aspect of His character and nature. Every one of His names is significant.[75]

His nature and personality is complex, wonderful, and deep. Yet a child can understand and relate to Him. In my many struggles as well as encounters with believers and skeptics, I have learned one thing. If you want to reject Him and make excuses of even His very existence, you will be able to do so—and many have. Remember, the Pharisees and the skeptics did not doubt the miracles. They discredited His "holiness" (because He dared to heal on the Sabbath) or the "source" of His power (accusing Him of sourcing from Beelzebub—that is, the devil). So even after presenting the most compelling scholarly and scientific evidence on Christ, the doubters, skeptics, and those who struggle with their own spirituality will find excuses and reasons.

These do not change the facts.

Jesus Christ is who He claims to be. He is the same yesterday, today, and forever.

So, what are the pragmatic recommendations for this most important chapter? Well, get to know Him. The best source is the scripture. Start with the Gospel of John. Make sure you understand He is the only one that stands in the gap between you and God. Your good works or efforts; even your scholarly research will not lead you to fulfillment or the truth. Only through believing and accepting Him will you be complete. You will be surprised by joy—as I and countless others have. You will gain purpose for your life.

---

[75] https://bibleresources.org/names-of-jesus/

Soon after I accepted Christ, I got involved with The Navigators ministry, and they discipled me. I am eternally grateful. One of the powerful tools from The Navigators is the "Bridge Illustration."[76] It clearly depicts the work of Jesus and how, through Him, you can have an abundant and eternal life.

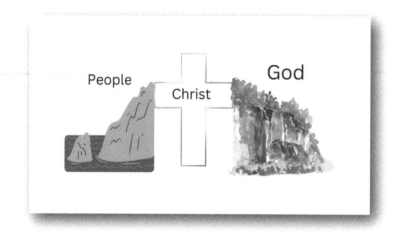

Blaise Pascal, the French philosopher and mathematician, said:

> There is a God-shaped vacuum in the heart of every man which cannot be filled by any created thing, but only by God, the Creator, made known through Jesus.

The fact is that by nature we like to go our own way. Not that we are happy or are satisfied when we are self-centered or attempt to be self-sufficient. St. Augustine said: "Our hearts are restless until they rest in Thee."

We are rebellious. We like to do things our own way—often with dismal consequences. We try to push God out of the picture. We try to fill our lives with all kinds of junk, none of which satisfies. We are restless; nothing can satisfy us except a dynamic relationship with God. We try to fill our emptiness with material things, relationships, and pleasure. They all fall short. Also, we do not know how to find our rest in Him.

---

[76] https://www.navigators.org/wp-content/uploads/2021/02/navigators-bridge-to-life.pdf

Seven hundred years before Christ, the prophet Isaiah spoke about being like sheep—going our own way and doing our own thing, as it says in Isaiah 53:6a (The Message):

> We're all like sheep who've wandered off and gotten lost.
>
> We've all done our own thing, gone our own way.
>
> And that includes all of us—no exceptions.

It is reiterated in the New Testament:

> For all have sinned and fall short of the glory of God. (Romans 3:23)

The fact is, God does have a wonderful plan for our lives, but we cannot enjoy it in our sinful state.

There are always consequences to our actions. The Word of God says the wage of sin is death. *Wage* here means the consequences, the price that we pay for our sinfulness.

> For the wages of sin is death, but the gift of God is eternal life in Christ Jesus our Lord. (Romans 6:23)

What is death? Death means separation. It is similar to a broken relationship. Sin has broken and continues to break our relationship with God. Again, the prophet Isaiah reflects this separation:

> But your iniquities have separated you from your God; your sins have hidden his face from you, so that he will not hear. (Isaiah 59:2)

So, in order to respond to our restlessness and this deep separation from eternity as well as the eminence of the ultimate separation, death, we try to reach the skies and have a sense of immortality. We have built monuments and attempted to achieve eternity through different means. We try to make a name for ourselves. We try to be good to others. We try to balance our good deeds and justify to ourselves why we deserve to be immortal and acceptable in the presence of God. The fact of the matter is that we always come short. The Word of God is quite blunt about it:

> All of us have become like one who is unclean, and all our righteous acts are like filthy rags; we all shrivel up like a leaf, and like the wind our sins sweep us away. (Isaiah 64:6)

It is not a pretty picture. We imagine and hope our national heritage, our baptism, even our church attendance, volunteer efforts, our monetary or charitable contributions will somehow save us. But alas! They all come short.

However, everything we do comes short. We cannot reach to the stars, let alone God. In fact, through our means, we have been quite pathetic.

The Lord has already taken the initiative and provides the ultimate answer for us.

> For it is by grace you have been saved, through faith—and this not from yourselves, it is the gift of God—not by works, so that no one can boast. (Ephesians 2:8-9)

The Word of God says we have been saved "by grace." What is grace? Grace is an unmerited gift. It is a gift we do not deserve, nor have we earned it. It is free but not cheap. Someone did pay a very high price for this gift to be ours. But it is free, and all we must do is accept this wonderful gift. It is starting to sound like good news, isn't it? It is like going to a patisserie and trying to purchase the most delicious cake, only to discover we do not have enough money to buy it. Then comes a stranger and buys it for us and gives it to us; we did not really know who this stranger is or what we have done to deserve this gift. All we must do is accept it! It is not our own doing. It is not our own talents. It is a gift.

So far we have seen our condition and what Christ did for us. In fact, the Word of God reemphasizes the work of Christ throughout the Bible:

> For God so loved the world that he gave his one and only
> Son, that whoever believes in him shall not perish but have
> eternal life. (John 3:16)

How about our response? Just because Christ was given for us is not enough. The second part of the verse makes it clear: this wonderful news is available to those who *believe* in Him.

What does it mean to believe in Him? It means to acknowledge our sinfulness, our separation from God, our inability to have meaning and purpose in our lives, the futility of our efforts in making us "righteous" and recognize that we are in a state of hopeless rebelliousness against God. Once we recognize this fact, we then turn to Christ and accept His work on the cross—in other words, believe in Him as God incarnate, perfect man and perfect God, who came and died for our sins. Remember what we said earlier about sin? Someone must pay the price of our sin (the "wages"). Well, Christ paid that price with His life. Our responsibility and response is to believe in this fact and raise our empty hands of faith and receive it. That's all.

> For there is one God and one mediator between God and
> men, the man Christ Jesus. (1 Tim. 2:5)

So we need to believe in His mediation: Jesus Christ dying on the cross for us, for our sins to reconcile us to God. That is all the "work" that we need to do in order to enjoy reconciliation with God. And this is the only way we will find acceptance, purpose, and restoration in our relationship with God.

Today and, in fact, right now, this good news could be a reality for you. Just knowing about it is not enough. You can now believe and surrender your life to God. Here is a simple prayer:

> Dear Lord, I acknowledge my sinfulness, I recognize that all my efforts in reaching you, finding purpose in my life have been futile. I believe you died and were resurrected to bring reconciliation between me and God. You, in fact, took the penalty of *my* sin on you. Please come into my heart and make me a new creation.

If you pray this prayer and believe it in your heart, you indeed will be reconciled with God. He will give you a new life and a new purpose. He will fill the vacuum that you have in your heart. You will have joy as you have never experienced before. And all this is a free gift—free but not cheap. If you want to enjoy this abundant life, be assured of your relationship with Christ, and find out more, scan the QR code:

4. The Burning Bush of the Word of God

4.1. Introduction

The Word of God—the Bible—continues to be the most read book in history.[77] It is the foundation for the Jewish (Tanakh, basically the Old Testament) and the Christian faiths (Old and New Testaments). Though less known, the Bible is also considered holy by Muslims, and they are encouraged to read it.

Jesus Christ is also identified as the Word of God—the Logos. He is God. So, the Word of God is identified with Christ, communicating and revealing God and bringing us close to God.

When I was a young Christian in the 1970s, I loved reading and studying the work of Dr. Francis Schaeffer. I loved mathematics and philosophy. It was so helpful to have a thought leader of his caliber help me navigate the very many trends that even then were shaping both the West and the East. Here is a quote from one of his famous books, *He Is There and He Is Not Silent:*[78]

> I find that many people who are evangelical and orthodox see truth just as true to the dogmas, or to be true to what the Bible says. Nobody stands more for the full inspiration of Scripture than I, but this is not the end of truth as Christianity is presented, as the Bible presents itself. The truth of Christianity is that it is true to what is there. You can go to the end of the world and you never need be afraid, like the ancients, that you will fall off the end and the dragons will eat you up. You can carry out your intellectual discussion to the end of the discussion because Christianity is not only true to the dogmas, it is not only true to what God has said in the Bible, but it is also true to what is there, and you will never fall off the end of the world! . . . We need the full biblical position to have the answer to the basic philosophical problem of

[77] https://www.businessinsider.com/the-top-10-most-read-books-in-the-world-infographic-2012-12

[78] https://www.amazon.com/He-There-Not-Silent/dp/084231413X

> the existence of what is. We need the full biblical content
> concerning God: that He is the infinite-personal God, and
> the triune God.

The Bible[79] is the truth that enlightens us holistically to understand the reality of existence, who we are, and how we should live: holistically.

The previous chapter elucidated the many ways different individuals and organizations have attempted to discredit Jesus Christ. If you want to destroy a religion or a movement, discredit its leader. Despite all these attempts—from the so-called scholastic such as the Jesus Seminar to the more grotesque such as the Communist Chinese government's "translation" of the Bible to depict a different Jesus—they have all failed.

It is therefore not surprising to note that the attacks on Jesus often go together with the attacks on the Word of God—the Bible.

There are so many misunderstandings and misrepresentations of the Bible that have become often ingrained in the psyche of the society. Here again, there are outright, well, liars who misrepresent the truth to scholars who have taken a very narrow and negative position toward the inspired Word of God.

Sometimes Christians—especially evangelicals—have a very defensive stand toward the Bible, especially given the constant attacks on the validity and reliability of the Holy Book.

The *Bible* has many designations and synonyms. We elucidate some of them in the following sections, starting with *Byblos*.

4.2. Byblos

As a Lebanese, one of the coastal cities we loved to visit was Jubail, the ancient *Byblos*.[80] Being a historic city—like most cities in Lebanon—

---

[79] Throughout I will use the Bible to mean the *Holy Bible:* God's Word that is sacred.

[80] https://en.wikipedia.org/wiki/Byblos

it had a lot to offer: cultural events, historic sites, and my favorite, some great coastal restaurants!

Byblos is where the Phoenician alphabet was created, and the name of the city means "book."

Byblos has a very rich history and profound associations with biblical themes and several Burning Bushes as we shall see. Here is a brief:[81]

> According to the historian Durant, "Byblos thought itself the oldest of all cities; the god El had founded it at the beginning of time, and to the end of its history it remained the religious capital of Phoenicia." Because papyrus was one of the principal articles in its trade, the Greeks took the name of the city as their word for book—biblos—and from their word for books named our Bible—ta biblia—which means "the books." Byblos is among the cities listed as candidates for the distinction of "oldest city in the world" as it has been continuously inhabited for over 7,000 years. Byblos is listed by UNESCO as a World Heritage Site.

---

[81] https://www.worldhistory.org/Byblos/

Therefore, this is where the word *Bible*—"the book"—comes from:

> The word Bible itself is simply a transliteration of the Greek word bíblos (βίβλος), meaning "book." So, the Bible is, quite simply, The Book.[82]

4.3. The Breath of God

Byblos is a coastal city in Lebanon, a unique country that is, at its core, sectarian: an aggregate of Christians and Muslims ruled through power-sharing arrangements. Since its independence in 1943, Lebanon has had numerous devastating civil wars and conflicts. One of the minorities that thrived in Lebanon was the Armenian community that, at one point, constituted 10 percent of the Lebanese population. Lebanon was a generous host country that, like many other Arab countries, especially Syria, received the Armenians who were the survivors of the first genocide of the twentieth century in 1915.

Historically, Armenians[83] have lived in what is now known as eastern Turkey and the Caucasus that was part of the Soviet Union. Most of Armenia is still occupied by Turkey, who refuses to recognize the Armenian genocide. Armenia is surrounded by hostile countries— especially Azerbaijan[84] and Turkey—and frequently faces economic hardships and is frequently at risk of existential threats.

---

[82] https://www.biblestudytools.com/bible-study/explore-the-bible/what-does-bible-mean.html

[83] There are close connections of Armenians to the Bible. Armenians are the people of Mt. Ararat, where Noa's ark rested. The area around Mt. Ararat is historic Armenia, and Ararat remains a symbol of endurance and hope for the Armenian people.

[84] As I write these words, Azerbaijan—with full approval and support from Turkey—has been blockading and trying to starve the Armenian enclave called Artsakh (aka Nagorno Karapagh): population of 120,000. The ethnic cleansing continues: https://www.christianitytoday.com/news/2023/january/nagorno-karabakh-christmas-blockade-armenia-artsakh-lachin.html

Armenians are the first nation in the world that became Christian as a nation in AD 301. At that time, Armenians did not have an alphabet, and the Bible that was in use was Syriac[85] and Greek. However, according to Armenian tradition, miraculously, a priest named St. Mesrob Mashdots[86] discovered the Armenian alphabet[87] and translated the Bible into Armenian.

The source manuscripts of the final Armenian translation were excellent, and the Armenian Bible—in addition to Syriac and other texts—is often cited as a reliable reference.

Armenians call the Bible *the breadth of God*, which of course comes from 2 Timothy 3:16. It is the only nations that use this designation of the Bible.

> All Scripture is God-breathed and is useful for teaching, rebuking, correcting and training in righteousness.

---

[85] Syriac is an ancient Aramaic dialect that had its own alphabet: https://en.wikipedia.org/wiki/Syriac_language

[86] https://www.britannica.com/biography/Saint-Mesrop-Mashtots

[87] There are scholars who believe the Armenian alphabet is much older and has evolved over centuries; see for example: https://ia801904.us.archive.org/32/items/alphabets-of-life/Scholars_Edition_Vol_1.pdf

The Bible is full of life and light. It frees, it guides, and it gets us closer to God and to one another. The invention of the alphabet and the translation of the Bible into Armenian had a profound spiritual as well as cultural impact on Armenians:[88]

> In consolidating Armenian identity, conversion includes proselytization and evangelism, whereas Christianization can be described as a cultural process, perpetuating an agency in the reshaping, reimagining, and remaking of culture. This Christianization for Armenia necessitated the creation of a script in what became the bearer of literary culture and a distinct ethno-religious identity. The advent of this alphabet and its rapid spread allowed for the Armenian people to preserve their teachings and traditions. The 36-letter alphabet (two more were added in the eleventh and twelfth centuries), created by St. Mesrop Mashtots, became so well-suited to the sounds of the Armenian language that it has served its purpose for over sixteen hundred years. The invention of an Armenian script untethered the intellectual and spiritual potential of an entire people, assisting in the cultivation of Armenian culture and preventing it from any susceptibility to amnesia.

4.4. Scripture

Another term that is used quite often to designate the Bible is *scripture*. It simply means "sacred writings or religious writings" and can apply to any religion. For Christianity, *scripture* is used to denote the Bible. In John 5:39, Jesus said:

> You study the Scriptures diligently because you think that in them you have eternal life. These are the very Scriptures that testify about me.

---

[88] https://providencemag.com/2022/01/breath-god-short-history-armenian-alphabet/

He was, of course, referring to the Old Testament. After the completion of the Bible through the inclusion of the New Testament, *scripture* now designates both the Old Testament and the New Testament.

In addition to being a synonym for the *Bible*, the term *scripture* has a deeper meaning as described by J. I. Packer in his article "Inspiration of the Bible" (published in *The Origin of the Bible*[89]):

> Scripture is not only man's word—the fruit of human thought, premeditation, and art—but also and equally God's word, spoken through man's lips or written with man's pen. In other words, Scripture has a double authorship, and man is only the secondary author; the primary author, through whose initiative, prompting, and enlightenment, and under whose superintendence each human writer did his work, is God the Holy Spirit.

4.5   The Word of God

In addition to the *breath of God*, perhaps the most profound characterization of the Bible is the *Word of God*. Why? As noted above, Jesus Christ—the second person of the Trinity—is himself, the Word:

> In the beginning was the Word, and the Word was with God, and the Word was God. He was with God in the beginning. Through him all things were made; without him nothing was made that has been made. In him was life, and that life was the light of all mankind. The light shines in the darkness, and the darkness has not overcome it. (John 1:1–4)

Jesus Christ *is* in the Greek original *Logos* λόγος, which is also the root of the word *logic*. The Word of God is His rational communication

---

[89] https://www.christianbook.com/the-origin-the-bible-updated-edition/f-bruce/9781414379326/pd/379321

through language. The universe was created by the Word of God (Hebrews 11:3). He is the agent and the cause at the same time. Our Lord Jesus Christ—being both perfect man and perfect God, the second person of the Trinity—is also the bridge (the rational communication) between humanity and God, the Word of God!

4.6.   The Testaments or Covenants

Christians are most familiar with the division of the "Old" and "New" Testaments of the Bible. According to Geisler and Nix in *A General Introduction to the Bible:*[90]

> The Hebrew word for *testament* is *berith*, meaning a "covenant, or compact, or arrangement between two parties." The Greek word *diathēkē* is often translated "testament" in the King James Version. This is a poor translation and is one of the corrections made in newer versions of the Bible that regularly translate it as "covenant." The Greek version of the Old Testament, the Septuagint (LXX), translates the Hebrew word *berith* as *diathēkē*, thus showing the derivation of the Greek term. The Old Testament was first called the covenant in Moses's day (Ex. 24:8). Later, Jeremiah announced that God would make a new covenant with His people (Jer. 31:31–34), which Jesus claimed to do at the Last Supper (Matt. 26:28, cf.; 1 Cor. 11:23-25; Heb. 8:6-8). Hence, it is for Christians that the former part of the Bible is called the Old Covenant (Testament), and the latter is called the New Covenant.

Here also, there is a much more profound semantics associated with *testament* or *covenant*, from a Middle Eastern perspective. While studying various topics, my wife, Silva, introduced to me a book that she found quite impactful: *The Blood Covenant.*[91] We both

---

[90] https://www.amazon.com/General-Introduction-Bible-Norman-Geisler/dp/0802429165

[91] https://www.amazon.com/Blood-Covenant-Story-Gods-Extraordinary/dp/0834130912

learned a lot from this anointed book. In fact, I studied the subject and ended giving couple of seminars on it. Here is how the authors Garlow and Price describe blood covenant:

> The Hebrew word for covenant is *berith* or *b'rit*, which simply means "to cut, to bind together in obligation." It is used nearly three hundred times in the Bible and comes from the root word meaning "to cut." But a more expanded definition of the word "covenant" is required to gain a rich understanding.
>
> Covenant is
>
> - an all-encompassing agreement between two parties with clearly outlined perimeters and promises,
> - a mutual understanding between two persons who bind themselves together with specific obligations to fulfill,
> - the giving of oneself or a group of individuals into a lasting union together for life and unto death,
> - entered into so as to complement strengths and weakness (never based on unilateral similarities),
> - a tangible expression of love and trust, and
> - a relationship that will require blood to be shed to reinforce the solemnity and seriousness of the bond.

They continue to explain and elaborate on the *blood* covenant:

> A covenant bond is very different from a contract agreement. How so? A contract is limited to the giving of goods, services, and products to another party. These terms may be negotiated or cancelled. What's more, contracts are made with ink. Covenants are made with blood and involve the giving of one's complete self to another—much more than just goods, services, or products!

> The difference between a covenant and a contract cannot be overstated. Another way of looking at it might be to say that a blood covenant's obligations overwhelm the requirements of a contract, but a contract's requirements can't hold a candle to the obligations of a blood covenant.
>
> These definitions explain why covenant is the highest and most honored expression of a relationship possible between two parties.

Of course, the ultimate blood covenant is the blood of our Lord Jesus Christ shed for us and through which we can be sealed through the Holy Spirit. The entire history of mankind and, more importantly, the salvation of mankind hinge upon this covenant. *This* is the New! There is no other "covenant" that can provide meaning or salvation to humanity. There is no other name under heaven through whom we can be saved. There is no other means to guarantee our eternal bliss than through the covenant of Jesus's blood.

This is the New Covenant—the New Testament!

4.7.   Inspiration of the Bible

As we noted above, Armenians (the only nation as far as I know) call the Bible the *breath of God*, which comes from 2 Timothy 3:16. God's breathing is the *inspiration* God has given to prophets and apostles to create the Old and New Testaments' canons, which will be discussed in the next section.

Here is an excellent explanation on inspiration and the outbreathing of God:[92]

> As we're nearing the end of our Why Bible series—a journey through the New and Old Testament and how we can apply it to our lives—it's important to truly understand what Paul

---

[92] https://kensingtonchurch.org/the-bible-is-god-breathed-what-does-that-really-mean/

was referencing when he wrote that "all scripture" is God-breathed. To understand the origins, allow me to teach a quick lesson in Greek.

The Greek word for "God-breathed" or as some translations say, "breathed out" is "theopneustos," which means "inspired by God" or literally the very "breath of God."

It can be a little misleading if we consider the modern meaning of inspiration, which can be defined as a creative impulse. But when we use the word inspiration in reference to Scripture, think divinely guided or divinely inspired. We believe that each word in the Bible originated from the heart of God, written by men who were inspired by the Holy Spirit to write down exactly what God wanted to communicate to us.

The Apostle Peter explained it this way:

Above all, you must understand that no prophecy of Scripture came about by the prophet's own interpretation of things. For prophecy never had its origin in the human will, but prophets, though human, spoke from God as they were carried along by the Holy Spirit. (2 Peter 1:20–21)

The source of the breathing is God, but it is not "possession." God does not crush or annihilate the personality of the authors. Their background, character traits all come through, even though the source is God. Yes, its origin is God, but its manifestation is through the personality of the human without possessing or destroying him.

There have been and will continue to be a spectrum of interpretations to this most critical notion of inspiration and the amazing collaboration between God in the person of the Holy Spirit and man to produce the masterpiece we call the Bible. A Bible has been a bestseller for generations and withstood so many attacks and criticisms.

Chapter 2 of *A General Introduction to the Bible*[93] delves deep into Revelation and interpretation and provides a comprehensive elucidation of the different perspectives on this very critical topic. Here is how the authors describe this dynamic collaboration between God breathing—inspiring—and man writing the word (quoting primarily J. I. Packer for this particular point):

> The prophets played an important role in the overall process of inspiration; they were the means by which God spoke. The word of God was written by men of God. God used persons to convey His propositions. In other words, as J.I. Packer perceptively observes, there God exercised "*concursive operation* in, with and through the free working of man's own mind." He amplifies the concept further saying, We are to think of the Spirit's inspiring activity, and, for that matter, of all His regular operations in and upon human personality, as (to use an old but valuable technical term) *concursive*; that is, as exercised in, through and by means of the writers' own activity, in such a way that their thinking and writing was *both* free and spontaneous on their part *and* divinely elicited and controlled, and what they wrote was not only their own work but also God's work.

This dynamic, creative, respectful cooperation between the Holy Spirit and the human authors of scripture is unique to Christianity. It is very profound and reflects the wonderful and unique character of our Creator. He respects the personality, creativity, background, education, and innovation of the author while preserving the inerrancy of His Word. God did not dictate His Word. A perfect message through imperfect messengers reflecting His perfection. The "concursive" operation is an amazing attribute of His divinity and how He operates through us, the imperfect vessels, to come up with the essential rational communication between humanity and divinity.

---

[93] https://www.amazon.com/General-Introduction-Bible-Norman-Geisler/dp/0802429165

4.8.   The Canons

The Bible inspiration is God breathing out His words through men who were inspired to write the scriptures. The Bible is not a single book. It is a library of books: the Old Testament has thirty-nine books, and the New Testament has twenty-seven books—for a total of sixty-six books. But how did we get these books? How did these books come together to constitute the Bible that we hold in our hands? Here is how the biblical scholar Bruce Metzger puts it:[94]

> The recognition of the canonical status of the several books of the New Testament was the result of a long and gradual process, in the course of which certain writings, regarded as authoritative, were separated from a much larger body of early Christian literature. Although this was one of the most important developments in the thought and practice of the early Church, history is virtually silent as to how, when, and by whom it was brought about. Nothing is more amazing in the annals of the Christian Church than the absence of detailed accounts of so significant a process.

The inspiration of the Bible pertains to call the *canon* of scripture: the precise sixty-six books. *Canon* is a Greek word that means "a rule, a standard." From F. F. Bruce's classic, *The Canon of Scripture:*[95]

> When we speak of the canon of scripture, the word "canon" has a simple meaning. It means the list of books contained in scripture, the list of books recognized as worthy to be included in the sacred writings of a worshipping community. In a Christian context, we might define the word as "the list of the writings acknowledged by the Church as documents of the divine revelation." In this sense the word appears to

---

[94] https://strateias.org/metzger.htm

[95] https://www.amazon.com/Canon-Scripture-F-Bruce/dp/083081258X

> have been first used by Athanasius, bishop of Alexandria, in
> a letter circulated in AD 367.
>
> The word "canon" has come into our language (through
> Latin) from the Greek word kancn. In Greek it meant a rod,
> especially a straight rod used as a rule; from this usage
> comes the other meaning which the word commonly bears
> in English—"rule" or "standard."

Most of us who read, listen to, memorize, or meditate on the various passages or verses of the Bible, we do not concern ourselves with the "canon" of the Bible and its history. Yet it is an amazing Burning Bush, from its creation to preservation.

Like the Burning Bush of our Lord Jesus Christ, it is not without its controversies and challenges. We will be highlighting some of it in this chapter. Dr. Denny Petrillo[96] elaborates on the canon:

> It is clear that there were numerous written documents
> during the times of the Bible, from the days of Moses in 1400
> B.C. to the end of the New Testament in 100 A.D. Among
> those documents were writings of a religious nature. Some
> of these writings even portray themselves as being written
> by inspired men. Yet those writings were not accepted as
> part of the canon, that is they did not measure up to this
> divine standard. But why? What was it that made those
> during these biblical centuries—the people during that
> era—reject these writings while accepting others? *Herein
> lies the interesting journey in discussing biblical canonicity.*
> [Italics added]

The books that are considered part of the Old Testament and those of the New Testament have each their development, history, and yes, their respective controversies. In the following sections we shall elaborate on some of these with references of excellent scholarly

---

[96] https://youtu.be/iAIAZd_7CQA

work that delves deep into each of these topics. As noted, there are controversies, and the canon of scripture does have essential and core commonality when it comes to the Catholic, Orthodox, and Protestant denominations. But they are not identical. More on that in a subsequent section.

4.8.1. *The Canon of the Old Testament*

The development of the canon of the Old Testament is complex and controversial. Before delving deeper into the history of how the Old Testament canons were development, I took for granted (rather naively, I should add, and without much thought) that we, as Christians, inherited the Old Testament canon from the Jews and added the New Testament books as canon (discussed in the next section). While at a very high level that is true, there is much more to the development of the Old Testament canon. The version of the Bible that I use most for my daily study and Quiet Time is the New International Version[97] (NIV).

The thirty-nine Old Testament books included in the NIV table of content is identical to the ones contained in the King James Version, which is very popular within Protestant churches. F. F. Bruce describes it as follows:

> The Authorized (King James) Version of 1611 was formally a revision of the last (1602) edition of the Bishops' Bible; it included a version of the Apocrypha as a matter of course. Four years later, the Archbishop of Canterbury, George Abbot, a firm Calvinist in theology, forbade the binding or selling of Bibles without the Apocrypha on penalty of a year's imprisonment. 22 This measure seemed to be necessary because of the increasingly vocal Puritan objection to the inclusion of the Apocrypha among the canonical books. In 1589 an attack on their inclusion by John Penry ("Martin

---

[97] https://www.biblestudytools.com/niv/

Marprelate") had called forth a spirited reply from an earlier Archbishop, John Whitgift. Now, despite the penalty enacted by Archbishop Abbot, copies of the AV/KJV without the Apocrypha began to be produced in the years from 1626 onward.

The tide was running in the Puritan favour in those years: in 1644 the Long Parliament ordained that the Apocrypha should cease to be read in services of the Church of England. Three years later the Assembly of Divines at Westminster introduced their historic Confession of Faith with a chapter "Of the Holy Scripture."

He then goes on to list the books that are familiar to most of us.

How did these books come to be accepted as the canon of the Old Testament? Was it the result of a majority vote, a dictate from a powerful authority, or decided by a council? Human reason, void of the divine out-breathing of God, of His Word through His prophets, will seek and justify a rational reason for the composition of the canon.

The reality is that the Old Testament and the New Testament (discussed next) were recognized as divine by the authentication of the prophets and the acceptance of the people of God through centuries—in fact, millennia.

Concluding the development (self-authentication) of the Old Testament canon, Giesler and Nix summarize it as follows:

There are three steps to canonization: (1) inspiration by God; (2) recognition by men of God; and (3) collection and preservation by the people of God. The history of the canon indicates a gradual development of the collection of prophetic books which were added continually to the Law as they were written.

The Old Testament canon was probably completed about 400 B.C., and perhaps by about 200 B.C. the twenty-two books that had undergone this process of canonization began to assume an alternate threefold classification: the Law, the Prophets, and the Writings.

Here are the Old Testament books in this classification:

- *The Law.* Also known as the Pentateuch, these are the first five books of the Old Testament: Genesis, Exodus, Leviticus, Numbers, and Deuteronomy.

- *The Prophets.* These include the following:
  - Former prophets Joshua, Judges, 1 and 2 Samuel, 1 and 2 Kings
  - Latter prophets: Isaiah, Jeremiah, Ezekiel, the Twelve Minor Prophets

- *The Writings.* These include Psalms, Proverbs, Job, the Song of Songs, Ruth, Lamentations, Ecclesiastes, Esther, Daniel, Ezra-Nehemiah (counted as one book), 1 and 2 Chronicles.

4.8.2. The Canon of the New Testament

Like the Old Testament canon, the New Testament canon also came to be recognized as the breathing-out of God's Word through apostles and prophets. The collection of books that we have in the New Testament canon was the result of a gradual process. The creation, acceptance, and propagation of the New Testament is another amazing miraculous Burning Bush.

The books of the New Testament: Matthew, Mark, Luke, John, Acts, Romans, 1 Corinthians, 2 Corinthians, Galatians, Ephesians, Philippians, Colossians, 1 Thessalonians, 2 Thessalonians, 1 Timothy, 2 Timothy, Titus, Philemon, Hebrews, James, 1 Peter, 2 Peter, 1 John, 2 John, 3 John, Jude, Revelation.

This is how Milton Fisher describes it in his chapter "The Canon of the New Testament" in the *Origins of the Bible:*[98]

> The historic process was a gradual and continuous one, but it will help us understand it if we subdivide the nearly three and one-half centuries involved into shorter periods of time. Some speak of three major stages toward canonization. This implies, without justification, that there are readily discernible steps along the way. Others simply present a long list of the names of persons and documents involved. Such a list makes it difficult to sense any motion at all. A somewhat arbitrary breakdown into five periods will be made here, with the reminder that the spreading of the knowledge of sacred literature and the deepening consensus as to its authenticity as inspired Scripture continued uninterruptedly. The periods are:
>
> 1. First Century
> 2. First Half of Second Century
> 3. Second Half of Second Century
> 4. Third Century
> 5. Fourth Century
>
> Again, without meaning to imply that these are clear-cut stages, it will be helpful to notice the major trends observable in each of the periods just identified. In the first period, of course, the various books were written, but they also began to be copied and disseminated among the church. In the second, as they became more widely known and cherished for their contents, they began to be cited as authoritative.
>
> By the end of the third period they held a recognized place alongside the Old Testament as "Scripture," and they began to be both translated into regional languages and made the subject of commentaries. During the third century A.D.,

---

[98] http://files.tyndale.com/thpdata/firstchapters/978-0-8423-8367-7.pdf

our fourth period, the collecting of books into a whole "New Testament" was underway, together with a sifting process which was separating them from other Christian literature. The final, or fifth, period finds the church fathers of the fourth century stating that conclusions regarding the canon have been reached which indicate acceptance by the whole church. Thus, in the most strict and formal sense of the word, the canon had become fixed. It remains to list in greater detail the forces and individuals which produced the written sources witnessing to this remarkable process through which, by God's providence, we have inherited our New Testament.

Therefore, the history of the development of the canon of the New Testament was a process. I believe—as do many other Christians—it was a *divine* process protected by the Lord himself. Of course, no one can prove that. But we can know it from the evidence. There is *life* in His Word. When the Lord spoke and explained the scriptures to two of His disciples after He was resurrected and after their eyes were opened, this is what they said in Luke 24:32:

Were not *our hearts burning* within us while he talked with us on the road and opened the Scriptures to us? (Emphasis added.)

The point and counterpoint on scripture will not be resolved this side of eternity. There are competent scholars who have been arguing for centuries. But here again, there is a God-Point. The God-Point is the testimony of the scripture itself: the testimony of the Holy Spirit burning in our hearts, where we know what we are reading came out of the breath of the Lord. Not too scientific or scholarly? I agree. Nevertheless, true at least from my own experience and walk with the Lord. When I was a young Christian, I fell in love with Him and His Word and started not only studying but also memorizing the Word.

Verses I have learned decades ago, I still remember, and they continue to impact my life. My heart burns. In addition to memorizing the verses in the Topical Memory System,[99] which I highly recommend, I ended up memorizing the entire book of Philippians. It is my favorite Pauline Epistle.

On a final note, on the development of the New Testament canon, Bruce M. Metzger, in his book *The Canon of the New Testament*,[100] is spot-on in being amazed by why we do not have a much better documented and detailed account of this process:

> The recognition of the canonical status of the several books of the New Testament was the result of a long and gradual process, in the course of which certain writings, regarded as authoritative, were separated from a much larger body of early Christian literature. Although this was one of the most important developments in the thought and practice of the early Church, history is virtually silent as to how, when, and by whom it was brought about. Nothing is more amazing in the annals of the Christian Church than the absence of detailed accounts of so significant a process.

4.9.   Bible Variances

The Bible is an amazing Burning Bush! Our Lord has preserved His Living Word for centuries.

However, it has controversies, and there are variations (though relatively minor) of the Bible that are used by different denominations. This side of eternity, the history of the development will continue to fill volumes with a spectrum of opinions. Nevertheless, for those who have been born by the Spirit, it will

---

[99] https://www.navigators.org/resource/topical-memory-system/

[100] https://www.amazon.com/Canon-New-Testament-Development-Significance/dp/0198269544

continue to burn our hearts. It is living, active, and sharper than a two-edged sword (Hebrews 4:12)!

The aforementioned sixty-six books of the Bible are considered the canon primarily by the Protestant denominations. They are included and used by the other denominations. However, when you consider the books of the Bible in the Catholic and Orthodox denominations, you will see differences. The evolution of the Bible and what we have in our hands as the Holy Scripture is both miraculous, amazing, yet complex and often controversial.

The additional books that are found in the Catholic and Orthodox Bibles are called *the apocrypha* by Protestants and often designated as *deuterocanonical* (which means "belonging to the second canon") by Catholics. According to Wikipedia:[101]

> Apocrypha are works, usually written, of unknown authorship or of doubtful origin. The word apocryphal (ἀπόκρυφος) was first applied to writings which were kept secret because they were the vehicles of esoteric knowledge considered too profound or too sacred to be disclosed to anyone other than the initiated. Apocrypha was later applied to writings that were hidden not because of their divinity but because of their questionable value to the church. In general use, the word apocrypha has come to mean "false, spurious, bad, or heretical."

> Biblical apocrypha are a set of texts included in the Septuagint and the Latin Vulgate, but not in the Hebrew Bible. While Catholic tradition considers some of these texts to be deuterocanonical, and the Orthodox Churches consider them all to be canonical, Protestants consider them apocryphal, that is, non-canonical books that are useful for instruction. Luther's Bible placed them in a separate section in between the Old Testament and New Testament called the Apocrypha, a convention followed by subsequent

---

[101] https://en.wikipedia.org/wiki/Apocrypha

Protestant Bibles. Other non-canonical apocryphal texts are generally called pseudepigrapha, a term that means "false attribution."

4.9.1.   The Catholic Bible

The Catholic Bible contains the additional deuterocanonical books. These are categorized in the Old Testament canon of the Catholic Bible. There are two main sources of Old Testament scripture: the Masoretic Hebrew Bible and the Greek Septuagint. The Catholic Bible uses both.[102]

The canon of the Old Testament books of the Catholic Bible is based on history. We didn't make up the list!

At the time of Jesus, there was no official canon of the books of the Old Testament. The process of defining that canon was not yet complete, and there were a few different collections of scripture in circulation among the Jews.

The two most widely accepted collections of Old Testament writings at that time were the following:

- The *Septuagint* was an early Greek translation of the Old Testament. It contained forty-six books:

  - Genesis, Exodus, Leviticus, Numbers, Deuterono-my, Joshua, Judges, Ruth, 1 and 2 Samuel, 1 and 2 Kings, 1 and 2 Chronicles, Ezra and Nehemiah, Tobit, Judith, Esther, 1 and 2 Maccabees, Job, Psalms, Proverbs, Ecclesiastes, the Song of Songs, the Wisdom of Solomon, Sirach (Ecclesiasticus), Isaiah, Jeremiah, Lamentations, Baruch, Ezekiel, Daniel, Hosea, Joel, Amos, Obadiah, Jonah, Micah, Nahum, Habakkuk, Zephaniah, Haggai, Zachariah, and Malachi.

---

[102] https://www.beginningcatholic.com/books-of-the-catholic-bible

- ■ Another collection of the Old Testament in Hebrew contained just thirty-nine books.

  - It omits Tobit, Judith, Wisdom, Sirach (Ecclesiasticus), Baruch, and 1 and 2 Maccabees.

  - It also omits chapters 10–16 of Esther and three sections of Daniel: Daniel 3:24–90, Daniel 13, and Daniel 14.

  - These books and chapters are called the *deuterocanonical* books, meaning "second canon."

Although Hebrew-speaking Jews at the time of Jesus would have used the Hebrew Old Testament, the Greek-speaking world around them used the *Septuagint*.[103] The authors of the New Testament's books also quoted directly from the Septuagint most of the time, and this version was the most used in the early Church.

Precisely because the Septuagint was the version most used and accepted in the Church's earliest days, the Catholic Church uses the Septuagint's canon of Old Testament books in the Roman Catholic Bible.

However, as described by Jimmy Akon, Catholic apologist and podcast host, it is not that straightforward. The sources and translation of the Catholic Bible, as well as Orthodox and Protestant Bibles, are more complex.[104]

Until recently, most Catholic versions of the Old Testament were translated (primarily) from the Latin Vulgate rather than from the LXX or the MT. They might be based on the Vulgate using the LXX and the MT for purposes of comparison (e.g.,

---

[103] The Septuagint is also known as LXX; this is the Roman number representing 70—tradition states seventy (sometimes seventy-two) Jewish scholars translated the Bible into Greek in around the third century BC.

[104] https://jimmyakin.com/2006/04/septuagint_or_m.html

to decide between disputed renderings), but the Vulgate was the base text used by most Western Catholics. (It's different among Eastern Catholics.)

The Vulgate was based on the (pre-Masoretic) Hebrew text, the LXX, and the Old Latin Version.

The canon of the Catholic Old Testament is based on the LXX, so that's the top level where the LXX is employed in making translations. (In the ancient world, both the LXX and the Hebrew scriptures had fuzzy boundaries about what books they included, but a few centuries after Christ, the Catholic Church settled on one LXX-derived canon, and in about the same timeframe, the Jewish community settled on one Hebrew canon, which was later used to prepare the MT.)

Some of the books of the Catholic Old Testament seem to have been written as part of the developing LXX tradition (e.g., Wisdom, 2 Maccabees), so there are no earlier versions. For these, Catholic translators use the LXX since there is no MT equivalent of these books.

Other books of the Catholic Old Testament were based on earlier versions in Hebrew or Aramaic but have survived primarily in the LXX (e.g., Sirach). For these Catholic translators tend to use primarily the LXX, but they may also consult the original language versions to the extent that these have been recovered by archaeology (e.g., the Hebrew version of Tobit).

Still other books are found in both the LXX and the MT. Here recent Catholic translators have tended to use the MT as their base text, using also the LXX and the Dead Sea Scrolls (DSS) for purposes of comparison.

In the Catholic Church, many services were conducted in Latin, using the Latin Vulgate of the Bible that many Catholics in different countries around the world did not understand. Throughout the centuries of the history of Christianity, there were persecutions when saints, following the prompting of the Holy Spirit, attempted to translate and make available the Word of God in the language of the commoners. The textbook example of this is Tyndale, who wanted to have the scripture in English. He was executed by the Catholic Church. From Wikipedia:[105]

> Tyndale's translations were condemned in England by Catholic authorities, where his work was banned and copies burned. Catholic officials, prominently Thomas More, charged that he had purposely mistranslated the ancient texts in order to promote anti-clericalism and heretical views. In particular they cited the terms "church," "priest," "do penance" and "charity," which became in the Tyndale translation "congregation," "senior" (changed to "elder" in the revised edition of 1534), "repent" and "love," challenging key doctrines of the Roman Catholic Church.

It gets even more interesting when we consider the various Orthodox Bibles. There are various Orthodox denominations: Coptic, Armenian, Ethiopian, Greek, to name a few. Though the sixty-six books are used in their Bibles, when it comes to apocrypha as well *other books*, there are differences.

To illustrate, we delve deeper into two very ancient churches and peoples: the Armenians (not surprising) and the Ethiopians!

4.9.2. *Armenian Bibles*

My background is Armenian Orthodox—we prefer to call it *Apostolic*.[106] I was baptized as an infant and married by an Armenian Orthodox *քահանայ* (a married priest) in Madison, Wisconsin. The

---

[105] https://en.wikipedia.org/wiki/Tyndale_Bible

[106] https://www.britannica.com/topic/Armenian-Apostolic-Church

ceremony took place in a Greek Orthodox Church. When I grew up—even today—much of the liturgy of the Armenian Orthodox Church was conducted in what is called *krapar*—ancient Armenian. It is like having the original King James English, but much older. It is beautiful but sometimes difficult to understand.

Armenians were the first nation in history that accepted Christianity as the national religion in AD 301. However, Armenians did not have an alphabet. The Christian literature was either Syriac or Greek. There were oral translations of Bible passages or Christian liturgy. But it is impossible to promote the gospel without the written Word in the Armenian language. But that was a challenge, since Armenians did not have an alphabet.

So, there were two challenges for Armenians:

- Invent the Armenian alphabet.
- Translate the Bible into Armenian.

This miraculous feat was accomplished in AD 436:[107]

> Armenia officially adopted Christianity early in the 4th century, traditionally in 301 AD. But it took another hundred years before the problem of rendering the Bible into the Armenian language was taken up. Armenian chroniclers maintain that the lack of the holy scripture in the local language was an obstacle to missionary work. In fact, the main motivation behind the creation of the Armenian alphabet itself by Mesrop Mashtots lay in having an Armenian Bible, which can be referred to as "the Holy Book" in the language ("*Sourp Kirk*" in Western Armenian pronunciation, or "*Sourp Girk*" in Eastern), but is more often called "*Astvatsashounch*" (Eastern) or "*Asdvadzashounch* " (Western)—"Inspired of God" being one way to interpret that in English. The first verse translated into Armenian was Proverbs 1:2.

---

[107] http://100years100facts.com/facts/armenian-one-first-languages-bible-translated

ՃԱՆԱՉԵԼ ՁԻՄԱՍՏՈՒԹԻՒՆ
ԵՒ ՁԽՐԱՏ ԻՄԱՆԱԼ
ՁԲԱՆՍ ՀԱՆՃԱՐՈՅ

čanač el zimasdud'iwn ew zxrad, imanal zbans hančaroy

TO KNOW WISDOM AND INSTRUCTION; TO PERCEIVE
THE WORDS OF UNDERSTANDING;
PROVERBS 1:2

There is evidence of both Syriac and Greek influence in the translation of the Bible completed by 436 AD into what we now call Classical Armenian, Grabar (or Krapar). It is often marked by scholars as "The Queen of the Versions" for its style and literal rendition of the original. The very first words written in Armenian, by tradition, come from the Book of Proverbs of the Old Testament: "To know wisdom and instruction; to perceive the words of understanding" (as the King James Version in English has it). The choice is not lost in the celebration of the Holy Translators, whose Armenian Church feast day in October is used to commemorate learning and at times to usher in the new school year, depending on a given Diaspora community's location. The Armenians may be the only people in the world who venerate translators in that way.

Although there are other relatively early versions of the Bible—such as those among Ethiopians, Copts, and Georgians, or the Old Church Slavonic translation—and bits and pieces were made into some local languages on occasion, it was another thousand years or so before the major languages that we think of today got to have their own translations of the Bible.

The miraculous discovery of the Armenian alphabet and then the subsequent translation of the Bible into Armenian were truly a golden age for Armenians not only spiritually but also culturally, as the Armenian alphabet spurred Armenian spiritual and secular literature.

There was a similar condition with the Armenian people. The spoken *vernacular* Armenian and the older *krapar* Armenian (the language of the Armenian Bible and the liturgy) became different so much so that often the commoners find it difficult to understand or write and communicate in the older Armenian. I remember attending Armenian Apostolic services in Beirut, Lebanon, in the 1960s and had real difficulty following the liturgy. Fortunately, that has changed, and now they are often more accessible. So, there was a gap in the language of the common people (the *vernacular* Armenian) and the language of the Church (the old *krapar* of the Armenian Bible and the Church's liturgy).

Enter the reformation and enlightenment of the nineteenth century.

There were now many educated Armenians—in Europe and elsewhere. Some, especially in the spiritual class, started to have an awakening. This was further encouraged by the presence of American missionaries who came to the Ottoman Empire to save few souls. As one of the Armenian evangelical authors puts it, there was a fertile ground of an Armenian harvest in Constantinople, "Restless souls . . . eager for learning, as well as for the reform of their Church."[108]

Missionaries Fisk, King, Bird, and Goodell (sent organically to evangelize the Muslims) were assigned to evangelize the Armenians as well. The converted Armenians soon faced resistance from the Armenian Apostolic Church and were forced to create a separate

---

[108] From Chopourian's book *The Armenian Evangelical Reformation Causes and Effects*, https://www.amazon.com/Armenian-Evangelical-Reformation-Causes-Effects/dp/B000M2L9DI

community—a *millet*—recognized by the Ottoman authorities. Here is how they grew:

- July 1, 1846: 40 members; 1,000 adherents
- December 31, 1946: 4 churches; 140 members; 19,000 adherents
- By 1914, there were 137 churches, 14,000 members, and 51,000 adherents

Within the Armenian community, the *Revival Radio TV*[109] puts the impact of Armenian revivals to five hundred thousand Armenians!

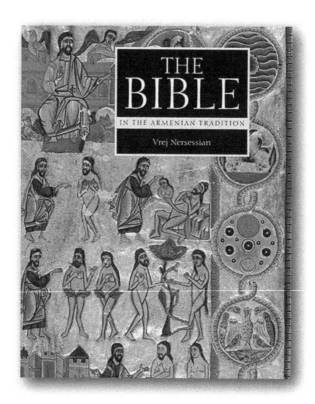

Dr. Vrej Nercessian, curator of Armenian Collections at the British Library, presents a compelling exposition in *The Bible in the Armenian*

Tradition.[110] The translation of the Bible to the Armenian vernacular was a major milestone in the spiritual revival of the Armenian nation. From Dr. Nercessian:

> Both Goodell and Buchanan stressed the devotion of the Armenians to the Bible, and both looked upon the Armenians not as a focus for Christian missions, but rather as assistants in the crusade to propagate the Christian faith throughout the world.
>
> Adger . . . completed his edition of the New Testament in classical Armenian with the Greek variants printed in Armenian in the margins. The Gospels, printed in Smyrna in 1837, were the first to appear, followed by the whole New Testament in 1838. Working with a number of Armenian assistants, Adger then revised the Zohrabian translation of the New Testament into modern Western Armenian, publishing the four Gospels in 1841 and the entire New Testament in 1842. *The Armenian-language printing of the Bible took on a new importance when the Armenian Protestant Community was formed in 1850, and hired the linguist and scholar Elias Riggs to prepare new editions. In 1853 the Smyrna press printed the complete Bible in modern Armenian.* (Emphasis mine.)

The Armenian nation, both from the ancient apostolic tradition as well as the evangelical reformed and revived Armenians, enjoyed the "living and active" characteristics of the Word of God (Hebrews 4:12). Spiritual, literary, and cultural life was imparted upon the nation through the Word of God!

4.9.2.1. The Bible Translations: Catalyst for Spiritual and Cultural Revivals

The invention of the Armenian Alphabet in the fifth century and the subsequent translation of the Bible in Armenian—the breath of God

---

[110] https://shop.getty.edu/products/the-bible-in-the-armenian-tradition-978-0892366408

as Armenians call it (and as far as I know, we are the only nation in the world that uses this appropriate name for the Word of God)— were not only a spiritual but also a catalyst for a national revival for Armenian sacred and secular literature:[111]

> Before the creation of their own alphabet, Armenians had an oral tradition which has come down to us under the general title of "SONGS OF GOLTEN." These oral traditions, epic tales, and legends preceded the creation of the alphabet in the year 406 A.D. by the monk Mesrob Mashdots, who was supported by Catholicos Sahag and King Vramshabuh. The conversion of the country to the Christian faith and the necessity of translating the scriptures and liturgy into the Armenian language accelerated the creation of the alphabet, which culminated in the total cultural independence of the Armenian nation.

> Despite the loss of political independence, the Armenian cultural identity was reaffirmed and secured, primarily in the fifth, or golden, century with the translation of the Christian and classic old literature. After a period of Iranian and Arabic influence, a Hellenistic influence became more evident in the seventh century.

> Following the highest expression of mystic literature with Saint Krikor Narektsi, there are some important contributions in the twelfth century, known as "the Silver Century." In addition to "Krapar" or classical Armenian, a new language, the Ramgoren or middle Armenian, appeared. This resulted in the creation of secular literature, especially by the troubador-poetic school, which was of great importance in the preservation of the national identity. In 1512, only 57 years after the invention of the printing press, the printed history of Armenia began. This fact, and the renaissance of culture and literature initiated

---

[111] Source referenced in http://www.lonweb.org/link-armenian.htm (Even though this is an excellent historical summary, unfortunately, the source has since been removed.)

by the Mekhitarian Fathers, culminated in the triumph of the modern Armenian language or Ashjarapar, which was entrenched by the end of the nineteenth century. This modern Armenian language became widespread in two variants: Eastern and Western Armenian, the first spoken in the Russian Empire and the second in the Ottoman Empire. Romantic literature was followed by the nationalist and realist movement (1880–1900), and this by the esthetic (1900–1915), and the symbolist.

There was a similar influence and golden age of Armenian literature, as the translation of the Bible into the vernacular gave the language a grammatical structure for high literature; the first Armenian vernacular grammar book was authored by an evangelical pastor. From Rev. Darakjian:[112]

> The translators worked out a peculiar grammar and syntax to be used for the translation. The evidence of this is shown in an article written by the renowned grammarian, Hovhannes Kazanjian (not an Evangelical) in the "Massis" newspaper, in 1907, where Kazanjian reveals that the first Armenian analytical grammar book was prepared and published by a Rev. Meguerditch Kirejian in 1863. Kirejian has also translated, most successfully, many hymns, some of which have found their way into our present hymn books.
>
> The translation of the Bible into Armenian vernacular was a giant step in the development of the Armenian literary language of the West, i.e. the western dialect. One of the great editors in those days, Puzant Kechian, calls the "Ashkharhapar" Armenian "the language of the Protestant." He also describes the language of the translation as "the purest and most popular and neat

---

[112] http://www.muncherian.com/r-barkevdarakjian-armenian.html Also check *Armenian Evangelical Movement: History, Faith and Mission*, https://www.amazon.com/Armenian-Evangelical-Movement-History-Mission/dp/1883131189/ref=sr_1_1

language in those days." Many renowned literary figures and linguists in Armenia and the diaspora acknowledge the fact that the translation of the Bible into the vernacular has no only enriched our literary language, but it actually contributed to the victory of the "askharhapar" over the "krapar," that is the old classical Armenian. Professor Vahe Oshagan calls the translation "the best both in volume and in quality." (Haigazian Armenological Review, ed. Dr. Yervant Kassouny; see the article "Arevmudahay Badmuvatzki Dzakoomu"—The Rise of the Short Story in the Western Armenian Dialect, by Prof. Vahe Oshagan; Beirut, 1971, p. 210.)

4.9.3. The Ethiopian Bible

The Ethiopian Orthodox Church is quite interesting and unique. In Acts 8:26–40, we read:

> Now an angel of the Lord said to Philip, "Rise and go toward the south[a] to the road that goes down from Jerusalem to Gaza." This is a desert place. And he rose and went. And there was an Ethiopian, a eunuch, a court official of Candace, queen of the Ethiopians, who was in charge of all her treasure. He had come to Jerusalem to worship and was returning, seated in his chariot, and he was reading the prophet Isaiah. And the Spirit said to Philip, "Go over and join this chariot." So Philip ran to him and heard him reading Isaiah the prophet and asked, "Do you understand what you are reading?" And he said, "How can I, unless someone guides me?" And he invited Philip to come up and sit with him. Now the passage of the Scripture that he was reading was this:
>
>> "Like a sheep he was led to the slaughter
>> and like a lamb before its shearer is silent,
>> so he opens not his mouth.

In his humiliation justice was denied him.

Who can describe his generation?

For his life is taken away from the earth."

And the eunuch said to Philip, "About whom, I ask you, does the prophet say this, about himself or about someone else?" Then Philip opened his mouth, and beginning with this Scripture he told him the good news about Jesus. And as they were going along the road they came to some water, and the eunuch said, "See, here is water! What prevents me from being baptized?" And he commanded the chariot to stop, and they both went down into the water, Philip and the eunuch, and he baptized him. And when they came up out of the water, the Spirit of the Lord carried Philip away, and the eunuch saw him no more, and went on his way rejoicing. But Philip found himself at Azotus, and as he passed through he preached the gospel to all the towns until he came to Caesarea.

From the tradition and history of the Ethiopian church, this was the beginning of the Ethiopian Orthodox church:[113]

Although Christianity became the official religion of the Aksumite kingdom in the fourth century, the religion had been known in Ethiopia since a much earlier time. In the Acts of the Apostles, VIII: 26–40, we are told of a certain Eunuch, the treasures of Queen Candace of Ethiopia, who went to Jerusalem to worship the God of Israel. There he met Philip the Deacon and was baptized by him. Ethiopian tradition asserts that he returned home and evangelized the people. In his Homily on Pentecost, St. John Chrysostom mentions that the Ethiopians were present in the Holy City on the day of Pentecost. Later, when the Apostles went out to preach the Gospel, Matthew was allotted the task

---

[113] https://www.ethiopianorthodox.org/english/ethiopian/prechristian.html

of carrying the good news to Ethiopia, where he suffered martyrdom. Ethiopian sources, such as the Synaxarium, make no mention of this, however; on the contrary, Ethiopians believe that received Christianity without shedding apostolic blood. Nevertheless, Christianity without certainly known in Ethiopia before the time of Frumentius, being the faith practiced by many of the merchants from the Roman Empire Settled in the Aksumite region. In important cities, such as Axum and Adulis, these Christian merchants had their prayer houses and openly practiced their religion.

The Ethiopian Bible is very interesting. It has more books than any other denomination. Depending on how the books are combined or counted, the number ranges between 81 and 88. Here is the classification:[114]

---

[114] https://www.euclid.int/papers/Anke%20Wanger%20-%20Canon%20in%20the%20EOTC.pdf

- ■ Books of Law (the Five Books of Moses)
  - Genesis
  - Exodus
  - Leviticus
  - Numbers
  - Deuteronomy

- ■ Books of History
  - Joshua
  - Judges
  - Ruth
  - 1 and 2 Samuel
  - 1 and 2 Kings
  - 1 and 2 Chronicles (2 Chronicles includes the Prayer of Manasseh)
  - Ezra and Nehemiah
  - Ezra Sutuel and 2 Ezra
  - Tobit
  - Judith
  - Esther
  - 1 Meqabeyan
  - 2 and 3 Meqabeyan
  - Joseph Ben Guriyon
  - Jubilees
  - Enoch

- Books of Psalms (Songs) and Wisdom
  - Job
  - Psalms
  - Proverbs
  - Reproof (*Tsegats* in Ge'ez)
  - Ecclesiastes Song of Songs
  - Wisdom (of Solomon)
  - Sirach

- Books of Prophecy
  - Isaiah
  - Jeremiah (including Lamentations, the Remainder of Jeremiah, and Baruch)
  - Ezekiel
  - Daniel (including Susannah, the Prayer of the Three Children, and Bel and the Dragon)
  - Hosea
  - Amos
  - Micah
  - Joel
  - Obadiah
  - Jonah
  - Nahum
  - Habakkuk
  - Zephaniah
  - Haggai
  - Zechariah
  - Malachi

From Beautiful Ethiopia:[115]

Ethiopian Bible is the oldest and complete bible on earth. Written in Ge'ez an ancient language of Ethiopia it's nearly 1,000 years older than the King James Version dating back to 300 to 500 AD and contains 81–88 books compared to 66. It includes the Book of ENOCH, Esdras, Buruch and all 3 Books of MACCABEE, and a host of others that was excommunicated from the KJV.

The astonishingly beautiful Garima Gospels are named after a monk, Abba Garima, who arrived in Ethiopia in 494, from Constantinople. Legend says he copied the Gospels in just one day because God delayed the sun from setting so the monk could finish his work. The incredible relic has been kept ever since in the Garima Monastery, near Adwa, in northern Ethiopia at 7,000 feet.

---

[115] https://www.facebook.com/ethiopiabeautiful

Of great interest is the inclusion of the Book of Enoch. The one discovered in the Dead Sea Scrolls and in the Ethiopian Bible is remarkably similar. Enoch is quoted in Jude. Though it is not in the canon of other denominations (Protestant, Catholic, or other Orthodox), it does provide further commentary and explanation to the Genesis 6 incident that created the giants. Furthermore, biblical scholars agree the Jewish as well as Christian fathers were familiar with it. From Timothy Alberino's *Birthright*:[116]

> In 1773, the famous Scottish adventurer James Bruce returned to Britain after living for six years in Abyssinia (known today as Ethiopia). During his travels, Bruce managed to acquire several copies of a manuscript that was once widely circulated in the ancient world but subsequently lost to history—the Book of Enoch. Unbeknownst to Western scholarship, the Ethiopians had preserved the manuscript and incorporated it into their canon of scripture. Thanks to Bruce, for the first time in centuries, scholars were able to read what many of the early church fathers considered to be the source material from which the opening verses in Genesis 6 were derived. Nearly two hundred years later, the fateful discovery of a young goatherd would confirm the authenticity of the Ethiopic Book of Enoch.

Here are other key observations from Albarino's seminal book:

- In 1947, a Bedouin boy discovered the Dead Sea Scrolls in a cave near the Dead Sea in Israel. The scrolls contained ancient manuscripts that had been hidden in jars for nearly 2000 years.

- The Dead Sea Scrolls consist of 981 texts written in Hebrew, Aramaic, Greek and Nabataean. They include copies of every

---

[116] https://timothyalberino.com/#book

book of the Hebrew Bible except Esther, as well as many other apocryphal and extra-biblical texts.

- One of the most significant apocryphal works found was the Book of Enoch, which provides more information about the biblical figure Enoch than is found in the brief Genesis account.

- The Book of Enoch presents Enoch as an eminent prophet and scribe. It suggests he authored works that were known to ancient Hebrews.

- The epistle of Jude quotes the Book of Enoch, confirming its status as an inspired prophetic work in ancient Jewish tradition.

- The discovery of the Dead Sea Scrolls provided unprecedented access to ancient biblical and extra-biblical manuscripts, expanding knowledge of Judaism and early Christianity.

We shall delve much deeper into giants, UFOs, and the Book of Enoch in volume 4. Suffice to say, the Burning Bushes are connected. Giants were mentioned not only in Genesis 6 but also throughout the Old Testament. Furthermore, the demons that Jesus cast out were the spirits of the giants—progenitors of the unlawful union of fallen angels and earthly women. Enoch 1 (especially chapter 6) provides further details on the fallen angel incursions! Our Lord Jesus Christ as well as the apostles and the early church fathers all knew the Book of Enoch.

4.10. Is the Bible Erroneous, Human Creation, or Corrupted?

The Bible is an amazing book that is alive and active. It changes lives and is the source of eternal life: Jesus Christ our Lord and the second person of the Trinity is identified as the Word of God.

However, it is not without controversies. The Old and New Testament canons have been transcribed and copied numerous times. Because the copying relies on fallible human scribes, errors and inconsistencies can naturally seep in. Often these are identified as footnotes or marginal notes in our Bibles. Probably we do not pay much attention if we read and study the Word on a regular basis, but most online and printed Bibles have them.

Accusations against the Bible claiming that the Bible was somehow changed or "corrupted" is nothing new. It has been going on for centuries and will continue until the return of the Word of God.

Elaborating on the erroneous, inaccurate, and outrageous claim by Dan Brown of *The Da Vinci Code*[117] that a council (e.g., Nicean, AD 325) decided the canon of the New Testament, ordered by emperor Constantine, Josh Peck elegantly highlighted the organic compilation of the canon:[118]

> The canon was historically compiled more in an organic fashion rather than being determined from carious councils.

The next two sections delve deeper into the challenges of the Bible from Islamic and Western ventages. When dealing with challenges to the Word of God, let us be scholarly and bold. Remember who the ultimate Author is! He knows how to protect His masterpiece! Challenges and attacks will continue!

I really like Daniel Wallace's warning and challenge:[119]

> It's disturbing that when it comes to the Christian faith, people don't really want—or know how—to investigate

---

[117] https://www.amazon.com/Vinci-Code-Robert-Langdon/dp/0307474275

[118] https://www.amazon.com/Lost-Prophecies-Qumran-2025-Final/dp/1948014483

[119] Daniel Wallace interview excerpt from *The Case for the Real Jesus*, https://www.amazon.com/Case-Real-Jesus-Journalist-Investigates/dp/031033926X

the evidence . . . Christians are not being led into proper historical research by their pastors. I have been saying for some time that I don't think the evangelical church has fifty years left of life to it until it repents. First, we have to quit marginalizing scripture . . . We can't treat the Bible with kid gloves. We really need to wrestle with the issues, because our faith depends on it. And second, we need to quit turning Jesus into our buddy. He's the sovereign Lord of the universe, and we need to understand that and respond accordingly.

4.10.1. *The Islamic Myth on the Corruption of the Bible*

Western Christians might be surprised to learn that the Quran encourages the faithful Muslims to read the Bible! In fact, our Lord Jesus Christ is called the Word of God, the Spirit of God, Messiah, and born of the virgin Mary—*in the Quran!*

Rev. Accad had studied Islam and the Quran for more than thirty years. As noted in the previous chapter, he came up with what was then called the "7 Muslim-Christian Principles," basically an expansion of Campus Crusade's Four Spiritual Laws but targeting Muslims, with quotes from the Bible *as well as the Quran* to lead Muslims to Christ. After my training, I used this amazing work and saw Muslims come to Christ with little or no resistance! The Quran is a bridge to Jesus Christ!

The Muslims are encouraged to read the Bible. In fact, Rev. Accad shares the Quranic verses that show the Islamic faith is based on the Bible and they need to go to it as a source. So why don't they? Why do the Muslims ignore the Bible? There are many reasons—some of them political and dealing with the centuries-old animosity between Muslims and Christians. Let's face it, nominal and materialistically or politically motivated "Christians," such as the Crusaders, are not that innocent - to say the least!

4-124 Dr. Setrag Khoshafian

Another reason is the creeping of the claim that the Bible got corrupted. This is key. We see modern versions of this, which will be covered below:

> What Does the Qur'an Say About the Injeel? Here is what the Qur'an says about the Injeel (the New Testament). Then we made our messengers follow them. We made Isa son of Mariam follow them, and we brought the Injil to him, and put compassion and mercy into the hearts of those who followed him. They invented monasticism. We did not ordain it for them, but only seeking Allah's pleasure. (Al-Hadid 57:27) We made Isa son of Mariam follow in their footsteps, confirming the Tawrat in his possession, and we gave him the Injil, in which is guidance and light, confirming the Tawrat in his possession, as guidance and an admonition to the reverent. (Al-Maida 5:46) When Isa brought miracles, he said, "I have come to you with wisdom, and to clarify to you your differences, so fear Allah and obey me." (Al-Zukhruf 43:63)

Rev. Accad then goes and debunks the claim that the Bible was corrupted with very well-thought-of and innovative arguments. First, he quotes several other verses from Quran, driving home the point that far from contradicting the Bible, the Muslims are encouraged on their foundation to uphold the Old (Tawrah) and New (Injil) Testaments:

> Do not argue with the people of the book but [speak] in a fair manner, except with the wicked among them. Say, "We believe in what was revealed to us and what was revealed to you. Our god and your god is one, and we submit to him." (Al-Ankabut 29:46)

> People of the book, you have no foundation unless you uphold the Tawrah and Injil and what was revealed to you by your Lord. (Al-Maida 5:68) In other words, Muslims are told to obey the Bible. Obviously, these verses show that Muhammad

did not think the Bible was corrupted in his time. Has it been corrupted since then, since the seventh century A.D.?

Then the coup de grâce is his innovative and on-point thesis on why the Bible is not corrupted:

Before Christ's time the Tawrat and Zabur existed in Hebrew, Greek, and partly in Aramaic. Also, before Muhammad's time at least part of the Bible had been translated in these additional languages—Syriac, Coptic, Latin, Armenian, and Gothic. In order for the Bible to be corrupted after Muhammad's time, the following events would have had to happen:

1. Representatives from every Jewish and Christian sect and denomination from at least seven or eight nations and languages, who were fighting with each other over controversial theological issues, would have needed to hold a conference and agree in detail on an explosive issue, namely, the changing of their Scriptures. (Of course, each sect would have wanted to change it to support the particular beliefs that split them in the first place.)

2. They would have had to agree on how to issue their new, corrupted version of the Bible.

3. They would have had to convince everyone who had a Bible in any language to exchange it for a new, corrupted version.

4. All the original Bibles would have had to be destroyed, leaving no evidence to succeeding generations. These events obviously did not happen. No one can supply the date and place of such a conference and name the participants and their resolutions. Historical records exist before Muhammad's time of events of far less importance. There is no documented evidence to validate such a history-changing event. In addition, many manuscripts exist from long before

Muhammad's birth in museums around the world. These manuscripts are the ones which the Qur'an affirms, and they are the ones from which current translations of the Bible are made.

Rev. Accad further adds:

In fact, the Qur'an seems to have foreseen such erroneous beliefs: They have good news in this world and in the hereafter: there is no exchanging Allah's words. That is the great victory. (Yunus 10:64) There is no exchanging Allah's words. (Al-Anaam 6:34) You will not find any substituting Allah's laws, nor will you find any changing of Allah's laws. (Fatir 35:43) The passages from the Qur'an in this chapter confirm the authority of the Bible, and confirm that the Bible has not been altered. This is a reassuring concept to those who have come to believe. The Qur'an is clearly on the Bible's side.

Quite compelling!

Let me add one more argument. The Quran is so clear about the Old and New Testaments' foundation of the faith and, of course, unquestionably the power of God. It is inconceivable to think the all-knowing and all-powerful God cannot protect the Word that He encourages His followers to read and base their faith on.

This is a rational argument that we can make to the Muslim believers. Is Allah incapable of protecting his Word in the Tawrah and Injeel? He is perfect! So of course, he could. The corruption is not on the side of God!

4.10.2. The Modern Myths on the Impact of Transcription Errors

In his seminal work *Revisiting the Corruption of the New Testament*,[120] Daniel Wallace delves deep into refuting especially sometimes

---

[120] https://www.amazon.com/Revisiting-Corruption-New-Testament-Manuscript/dp/082543338X

deliberate misinformation of omission of New Testament validity. Though there are variants and there could be minor transcription errors, the enormous number of manuscripts in many languages and with very early dates close to the lives of Jesus and His disciplines is an amazing Burning Bush.

> The average Greek NT MS is over 450 pages long. Altogether, there are more than 2.6 million pages of texts, leaving hundreds of witnesses for every book of the NT. It is not just the Greek MSS that count, either. Early on, the NT was translated into a variety of languages—Latin, Coptic, Syriac, Georgian, Gothic, Ethiopic, Armenian. There are more than 10,000 Latin MSS alone.

> No one really knows the total number of all these ancient versions, but the best estimates are close to 5,000-plus the 10,000 in Latin.

> It would be safe to say that we have altogether about 20,000 handwritten manuscripts of the NT in various languages, including Greek.

> If someone were to destroy all those manuscripts, we would not be left without a witness, because the church fathers wrote commentaries on the NT. To date, more than one million quotations of the NT by the fathers have been recorded. "[I]f all other sources for our knowledge of the text of the New Testament were destroyed, [the patristic quotations] would be sufficient alone for the reconstruction of practically the entire New Testament," wrote Bruce Metzger and Bart Ehrman.

> These numbers are breathtaking! . . . Far more important than the numbers is the date of the MSS. How many manuscripts do we have in the first century after the completion of the NT, in the second, and in the third? Although the numbers are significantly lower for the early centuries, they are still rather impressive. Today we have as many as 12 MSS from

the second century, 64 from the third, and 48 from the fourth.

You can check the highly scholastic articles from this impressive book. While there are variations and minor errors in transcriptions, essentially no core theology is compromised and the very act of preserving the Word is itself an incredible miracle—a Burning Bush. This was also brought home in Lee Strobel's excellent work *The Case for Christ*, especially his interview with Dr. Bruce M. Metzger. After proving the impeccable credentials of Dr. Metzger as a Bible scholar, Lee Strobel gets right to the point on the validity of the scriptures. Here are some of the answers from Dr. Metzger:[121]

> "What the New Testament has in its favor, especially when compared with other ancient writings, is the unprecedented multiplicity of copies that have survived."
>
> "Why is that important?" I asked.
>
> "Well, the more often you have copies that agree with each other, especially if they emerge from different geographical areas, the more you can cross-check them to figure out what the original document was like. The only way they'd agree would be where they went back genealogically in a family tree that represents the descent of the manuscripts."
>
> "OK," I said, "I can see that having a lot of copies from various places can help. But what about the age of the documents? Certainly, that's important as well, isn't it?"
>
> "Quite so," he replied. "And this is something else that favors the New Testament. We have copies commencing within a couple of generations from the writing of the originals, whereas in the case of other ancient texts, maybe five, eight, or ten centuries elapsed between the original and the earliest surviving copy.

---

[121] https://www.amazon.com/Case-Christ-Journalists-Personal-Investigation/dp/0310350034

"In addition to Greek manuscripts, we also have translations of the gospels into other languages at a relatively early time—into Latin, Syriac, and Coptic. And beyond that, we have what may be called secondary translations made a little later, like Armenian and Gothic. And a lot of others— Georgian, Ethiopic, a great variety."

"How does that help?"

"Because even if we had no Greek manuscripts today, by piecing together the information from these translations from a relatively early date, we could actually reproduce the contents of the New Testament. In addition to that, even if we lost all the Greek manuscripts and the early translations, we could still reproduce the contents of the New Testament from the multiplicity of quotations in commentaries, sermons, letters, and so forth of the early church fathers."

Biblical scholars are human. The Holy Spirit inspired them. But the Holy Spirit did not destroy their humanity. Even the minor typos are allowed to reflect, on the one hand, the inerrancy of the content of the scripture yet also allow for human frailty to coexist in a Living Word. An incredible—yes, breathtaking—Burning Bush!

4.11. The Gnostic Gospels

In addition to the apocrypha and other books such as the Enoch in the Ethiopian Bible's canon, there are "books" that pertain to a heretic sect that rose around the first and second centuries: Gnosticism. This heretic movement that many thought was quenched by the fifth century has made a comeback. Now it is manifested in various form of neo-Gnostic literatures. A prime example is *The Da Vinci Code*,[122] which we will expose in the next section.

---

[122] https://www.amazon.com/Vinci-Code-Robert-Langdon/dp/0307474275

In the documentary *The Gnostic Gospels Debunked*,[123] Professor Craig Evans provides a robust explanation of the movement:

> The Gnostics were a group that most scholars think emerged probably in the early second century some scholars have tried to argue that the group got underway a little earlier than that.
>
> The Gnostics were an interesting group a diverse group. So, we need to cautioned be cautious about lumping them all together as though they all fought and believed the same thing but these various groups of Gnostics from the Greek word gnōstikós—which means one who knows. So, there are the knowers of absolute truth—the precise opposite of agnostic a person who says ultimate truth can't be known well the Gnostics believed that they had it all figured out.
>
> One of the things they believed was that there actually were two gods there was the good god of light above who has nothing to do with this material world where we live and that there was an evil God who came about through an accident and this evil God made the world and holds us all captive in it and so the Gnostics claimed to have the knowledge the secrets on how to escape from this evil fallen material world and ascend up to the god of light and spirit above.
>
> They wanted to take Jesus and make him part of this program and so they interpreted Jesus as a almost like a spy or a secret agent who descends from the god of light above takes on a disguise and looks like an ordinary human and then fools the evil powers and fools the evil God and shows his followers his gnostic followers a way out of this bleak mess a way of salvation through knowledge the early church wisely sought from what it was a gross distortion with no credibility Jesus of course never taught these things. So these Gnostic writings were condemned and

---

[123] https://youtu.be/FCul_DB0zzw

> Gnosticism as a teaching was regard heresy and in time it faded away and disappeared.

This notion of the "other god" who is on our side should sound familiar to those who have studied New Age or Theosophy. As indicated in Wikipedia:[124]

> Within the system of Theosophy, developed by occultist Helena Blavatsky and others since the second half of the 19th century, Theosophical mysticism draws upon various existing disciplines and mystical models, including Neo-platonism, Gnosticism, Western esotericism, Freemasonry, Hinduism and Buddhism. ...

> "It is 'Satan who is the God of our planet and the only God,' and this without any metaphorical allusion to its wickedness and depravity," wrote Blavatsky, in *The Secret Doctrine*. "For he is one with the Logos." He is whom "every dogmatic religion, preeminently the Christian, points out as [...] the enemy of God, [... but is] in reality, the highest divine Spirit—Occult Wisdom on Earth. [...] Thus, the Latin Church [... and] the Protestant Church [... both] are fighting against divine Truth, when repudiating and slandering the Dragon of Esoteric Divine Wisdom.

There are several so-called Gnostic gospels with different levels of "Gnostic" philosophies. Several of them are frauds. From *Gnosticism Explained*,[125] some of the most important and fascinating Gnostic texts include the following:

- *The Secret Book of John.* An account of the creation of the world intended to serve as a sequel or prequel to the Gospel of John.

- *The Reality of the Rulers*. An exposition of the character of the archons by way of recounting and interpreting particularly telling episodes from the Gnostic creation myth.

- *The Revelation of Peter*. A story that strings together a series of revelations given by Christ to the apostle Peter, which famously features the Spirit of Christ laughing above the cross.

- *The Gospel of Philip*. A wide-ranging collection of parables, aphorisms, and other short pieces that contain some of the most often-quoted lines in Gnostic literature.

- *The Gospel of Truth*. A work of particular literary beauty that serves as a commentary on several early Christian writings that would eventually make their way into the New Testament.

- *The Gospel of Mary*. A version of the gospel story told from the perspective of Mary Magdalene, which unfortunately only survives in fragmentary form.

- *The Treatise on Resurrection*. An overview of the Gnostic perspective on salvation, emphasizing that it's an inner spiritual experience available in the present.

- *Three Forms of First Thought* and *Thunder, Perfect Mind*. Two ecstatic, revelatory, and highly enigmatic poems delivered from the perspective of a female divine being who may be Sophia and/or Barbelo / the Divine Mother.

- *The Gospel of Judas*. A version of the gospel story in which Judas is Jesus's favored disciple and in which Jesus discloses to Judas secrets of the universe and prophecies about horrible things the followers of Jesus will one day do in His name.

- *The Gospel of Thomas*. A collection of over a hundred sayings that attempt to guide the reader toward mystical union with Christ (and which might be a proto-Gnostic text rather than a truly Gnostic one).

4.11.1. *The Hoax and Fraud of* The Da Vinci Code

Many false statements are made in popular literature concerning the canon of the New Testament. One of the more outright—probably malicious—lies is the one made and popularized by the author of the *Da Vinci Code*, Dan Brown, that the canon of the New Testament was dictated and decided at the Nicaean Council by Emperor Constantine.

False!

Professor Bart Ehrman[126] provides the following perspective on the *Da Vinci* historic and factual inaccuracies:[127]

> Some of the historical claims about the non-canonical Gospels in the Da Vinci Code have struck scholars as outrageous, or at least outrageously funny. The book claims, for example, that some of these Gospels were discovered among the Dead Sea Scrolls. That of course is completely wrong: the Dead Sea Scrolls do not contain any Gospels, or any Christian writings of any sort. They are Jewish texts, which never mention Jesus or any of his followers. And the novel claims that Jesus' marriage to Mary Magdalene is frequently reported in the Gospels that did not make it into the New Testament. On the contrary, not only is their marriage not reported frequently, it is never reported at all, in any surviving Gospel, canonical or non-canonical.

Nicaean Council had nothing to do with a vote, discussion, or decision on which books were to be included in the New Testament. That is historically false!

---

[126] Professor Ehrman is an agnostic and atheist; nevertheless, he is a scholar who has done an impressive volume of work on biblical studies. We pray one day Professor Ehrman rediscovers his lost faith, repents, and returns to his Lord.

[127] https://ehrmanblog.org/jesus-mary-magadalene-and-sexual-innuendos

It is more serious than that. The book is not only filled with errors; it was stolen and plagiarized. Brown was sued for it. Brown had a neo-Gnostic agenda.

The Da Vinci Code—like much of the Gnostic theories—is based on historical errors and fiction in the imagination of the author. However, in case of *The Da Vinci Code*, it is much more serious. It was plagiarized form other sources. The book *The Da Vinci Fraud*[128] by Jack Dunn and Jonathan Coad provides the details. Here is the summary by Attorney Jonathan Coad:

> Ladies and Gentlemen of the Jury, I represent Jack Dunn in this case, whose stark claim is no less than that in writing The Da Vinci Code Dan Brown stole the plot, characters, themes and locations of his book The Vatican Boys. The issue before you is therefore one of plagiarism, for which the dictionary definition is: "The practice of taking someone else's work or ideas and passing them off as one's own." The question that you are asked to determine is whether in writing The Da Vinci Code Dan Brown plagiarized Jack Dunn's book, The Vatican Boys; and whether, apart from sections of Dan Brown's book which were taken from another book called The Holy Blood and the Holy Grail, much of the content of The Da Vinci Code has been taken from The Vatican Boys.

4.12.   Recommendations from the Burning Bush of the Bible

There are many reasons why the Bible is an amazing and perhaps one of the most important Burning Bushes. As noted above, the holy writ is not without its challenges, and the controversies that have persisted for centuries will persist until the return of our Lord.

But it is an amazing book: breathed out from God. Before delving more into some (impossible to do all) of the Burning Bush attributes of the Bible, let me add a personal note.

---

[128] https://www.amazon.com/Vinci-Fraud-Worlds-Greatest-Literary-ebook/dp/B09HCDYS6G

When Jesus appeared to two of the disciples after the resurrection, He explained the scriptures to them. Here is how St. Luke describes it:

> When he was at the table with them, he took bread, gave thanks, broke it and began to give it to them. Then their eyes were opened and they recognized him, and he disappeared from their sight. They asked each other, "Were not our hearts burning within us while he talked with us on the road and opened the Scriptures to us?"

This is key. As noted above, when I became a Christian in 1972, I was privileged to have been discipled by the Navigators.[129] This ministry emphasized one-on-one discipleship (reproducing through making disciples, as the Great Commission encourages us to do), especially through scripture memory (Topical Memory System[130] is just amazing and highly recommended) and Bible study. Through this ministry, I developed a tremendous thirst for the Word of God. I went beyond just memorizing the verses we were encouraged to memorize but also memorized the entire book of Philippians. Since then, the best time of my day is my morning quiet time in His Word.

Why is this important? Soon after becoming a Christian in my last high school year, I started studying mathematics (got a BSc and MSc) at the American University of Beirut. There were a number of required courses, and some of those were cultural studies. We studied historic books such as *The Epic of Gilgamesh*[131] and also some of the handbooks of the Bible. The point here is that it was not a religious course by any stretch of the imagination. Just another book among the many historical or significant cultural books worth studying. No "heart burning" there!

---

[129] https://www.navigators.org/topic/discipleship/

[130] https://www.navigators.org/resource/topical-memory-system/

[131] https://www.amazon.com/Epic-Gilgamesh/dp/014044100X

No matter how compelling the case for the Word God as His breath and rational communication (as Schaeffer would put it) to us, at the end of the day (take that literally!), if we are not regenerate and do not have a dynamic relationship with God, it will be, well, another cultural book. Interesting but hardly life-changing.

When it comes to the Word of God, the Bible, it is not enough just to *hear* some verses or passages of the Bible read during a Sunday sermon. That is good and important. But we need to also read, study, memorize, and meditate on the Word of God. One of the great illustrations that I thought when being discipled was the hand illustration on the Word:[132] the meditation was the thumb that held it all together. I have applied each finger of the hand illustration and have been blessed by it.

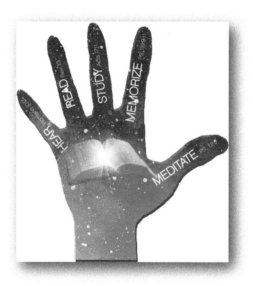

Here are the verses from the Bible instructing us to apply each of the fingers in the hand illustration:

- *Hear*. Consequently, faith comes from hearing the message, and the message is heard through the Word about Christ (Romans 10:17).

---

[132] https://www.navigators.org/resource/the-word-hand/

There are many opportunities to Hear the Word of God—especially through attending a Christ-centered biblical Church. There are also numerous online sources these days, but one should be careful as there are wrong and heretical teachings out there.

■ *Read.* Blessed is the one who reads aloud the words of this prophecy, and blessed are those who hear it and take to heart what is written in it, because the time is near (Revelation 1:3).

> The morning quiet time is the best time of my day, when I start the day reading the Word. I have been following a Bible through one-year plan for several years now, and it has been such a blessing.

■ *Study.* Now the Berean Jews were of more noble character than those in Thessalonica, for they received the message with great eagerness and examined the scriptures every day to see if what Paul said was true (Acts 17:11).

> Bible study, including small groups but also organized by Christian groups, is a true blessing to delve deeper in the Word and at the same time have fellowship. In addition to The Navigators and small church groups, I was involved as an attendee and leader in Bible Study Fellowship.[133] It was great, and I highly recommend it.

■ *Memorize.*

> How can a young person stay on the path of purity?
>
> By living according to your word.
>
> I have hidden your word in my heart
>
> that I might not sin against you. (Psalm 119:9, 11)

Memorizing scripture will bless your spiritual walk with God throughout your life. I went through the TMS as a

---

[133] https://www.bsfinternational.org/

young Christian, and till today, I recall and use the verses I had memorized. It is really the sword of the Spirit and can influence your spiritual battles and outlook on life.

- *Meditate.*

> Whose delight is in the law of the Lord,
>
> and who meditates on his law day and night.
>
> That person is like a tree planted by streams of water,
>
> which yields its fruit in season
>
> and whose leaf does not wither—
>
> whatever they do prospers. (Psalm 1:2–3)

Meditation is more work and requires discipline. There are techniques such as emphasizing different words in the verse, and see what you can glean from it. It is what holds the Bible together as you also meditate on how you can apply the Word in your life practically.

If you have the Holy Spirit in you, the Word of God (hearing, reading, studying, memorizing, and meditating) will give you joy. I have heard someone say the Word is life, our spiritual food, and prayer is our spiritual breath. I can testify to the reality of the rich indwelling and operation of the Word—accompanied by prayer—as absolute requirements for a healthy, fulfilling, and joyful spiritual life. To learn more and how you can dwell richly in the Living Word of God, scan the QR code:

5. The Burning Bush of Revivals

5.1.   Introduction

The history of Christianity is the history of revivals.

Like all movements, Christianity started with passion, fervency, and fire. But soon, stagnation and traditions took over, and the fire was quenched. Beautiful churches that were architectural marvels were erected—often with no life, suffocating legalism, and a spirituality that, at best, is wanting.

Christianity is radical, and Jesus Christ is the greatest revolutionary ever! Revival is about returning life (*reviving*) to individual believers, churches, or congregations that are—for lack of a better word—on life support or clinically dead and in need of resuscitation!

Without continuous revivals, Christian spirituality stagnates and dies.

The source, the power, the purpose, and even the duration of revivals is the Holy Spirit. Yet He chooses often imperfect people to move them to fan the flames of revival. One of the revivals in the beginning of the twentieth century was the Welsh Revival.[134] It started with a man of God, Evan Roberts, praying for change:[135]

> Evan Roberts who for twelve years cried out to God for a revival to change the condition of his country, Wales. Evan looked around him and saw that the country was, "as in the days of Noah." It seemed to him that the minds of the people were constantly on evil. Drunkenness, gambling, adultery, murder and theft were rampant. The moral decline of the land was on a downward cycle. And it was in the heart of this humble man that God imparted a burning vision for spiritual revival.

---

[134] https://www.bcwales.org/1904-welsh-revival

[135] http://reachournation.blogspot.com/2018/09/the-welsh-revival-of-1904-1905.html

Oh, how we need men like Evan Roberts for the twenty-first century. We are more similar to the days of Noah than the twentieth century. The flames of the great awakenings of previous centuries including the twentieth-century revivals have subsided, though there are sparks here and there.

Revivals answer the basic questions of meaning: why do we exist, what is our purpose on this planet, and how can we give it our all to accomplish it?

Revivals are always accompanied or even motivated by a realization of our shortcomings or the shortcomings of the Church.

It starts with repentance!

5.2. Revival Starts with Repentance

Our Lord's ministry and the ministry of John the Baptist started with *repentance.*

- *John the Baptist prepared the way for Jesus through the message of repentance.*

    > In the fifteenth year of the reign of Tiberius Caesar—when Pontius Pilate was governor of Judea, Herod tetrarch of Galilee, his brother Philip tetrarch of Iturea and Traconitis, and Lysanias tetrarch of Abilene—during the high-priesthood of Annas and Caiaphas, the word of God came to John son of Zechariah in the wilderness. He went into all the country around the Jordan, preaching a baptism of repentance for the forgiveness of sins. (Luke 3:1–3)

- *Our Lord Jesus Christ starts his ministry with the message of repentance.*

    > After John was put in prison, Jesus went into Galilee, proclaiming the good news of God. "The time has come,"

> he said. "The kingdom of God has come near. Repent and believe the good news!" (Mark 1:14–15)

- *The disciples and followers of Jesus continued with the message of repentance.*

> Peter replied, "Repent and be baptized, every one of you, in the name of Jesus Christ for the forgiveness of your sins. And you will receive the gift of the Holy Spirit." (Acts 2:38)

What is *repentance*, and why did John the Baptist and our Lord Jesus emphasize it? At its core, it's a change in direction: "Repentance is a 180-degree turn."[136] But what direction? Of course, the most obvious is the "turn" for those who were committing recognized sins, like tax collectors swindling money (e.g., Zacchaeus), or adulteresses, or murderers.

We encounter all types of repentance—turning, breaking down in regret, deep realization of one's sinfulness, following the Lord— in the New Testament and, in fact, throughout the history of the Church. Some are individual and dramatic, like the apostle Paul on the way to Damascus with letters to persecute the Church. In some cases, entire families repented. There are even reported cases of entire communities being saved. Similarly, in some cases (but not always), baptisms of the Holy Spirit and supernatural manifestations accompany revivals following repentance or turning to the Lord. Here again there is no single formula, and we should never put the Lord in a box or limit Him in an any way.

Repentance is the foundation that is often missing in most stagnant churches and communities. The routine and stagnated traditional behaviors and beliefs need to be rekindled through the fire of the Holy Spirit, starting with repentance.

It is not a popular topic.

---

[136] https://www.lockhaven.com/news/religion/2018/03/repentance-is-a-change-of-direction/

True repentance is often followed by baptisms and fillings of the Holy Spirit and even signs and wonders·. There are many different views on "baptism" vs. "being filled" with the Holy Spirit.[137]

I believe when you accept Christ, you are baptized through the Holy Spirit into the Church; you are "immersed" in it, and you become a Christian. Water baptism is your witness. Though I was baptized in the Armenian Apostolic Church as an infant, after accepting Christ, I got (water) baptized again—this time as a public testimony and witness of my Christian conversion. I did not get my second water baptism immediately at the time of conversion. I got it about a year later! Still after many years from my conversion and water baptism, I started to speak in tongues. It did not happen at conversion or my second water baptism. For some, it is immediate. There is no set rule.

Being filled with the Holy Spirit, on the other hand, is a continuous struggle. We should always aim to let the Holy Spirit control our lives.

However, emotional experiences and theologies on the Holy Spirit are not and should not be the driving force and starter of revivals. Repentance is. As we shall see, each revival is different. What is common is the accompanying repentance and return to a more dynamic and alive relationship with God.

A term that is often ridiculed and looked down upon in our postmodern society is "born again." We do not hear it as much today, and it is rarely preached from pulpits.

A person who repents gets born again and receives the Holy Spirit. Here is the biblical passage on being born again (John 3:1–8):

> He [Nicodemus—a Pharisee] came to Jesus at night and said,
> "Rabbi, we know that you are a teacher who has come from
> God. For no one could perform the signs you are doing if God

---

[137] The work of the Holy Spirit is a complex and controversial issue that has divided many churches and denominations. What I am sharing are my own beliefs and experiences. For a brief description, see https://www.crosswalk.com/church/pastors-or-leadership/ask-roger/the-baptism-and-filling-of-the-holy-spirit.html

were not with him." Jesus replied, "Very truly I tell you, no one can see the kingdom of God unless they are born again."

"How can someone be born when they are old?" Nicodemus asked. "Surely they cannot enter a second time into their mother's womb to be born!"

Jesus answered, "Very truly I tell you, no one can enter the kingdom of God unless they are born of water and the Spirit. Flesh gives birth to flesh, but the Spirit gives birth to spirit. You should not be surprised at my saying, 'You must be born again.' The wind blows wherever it pleases. You hear its sound, but you cannot tell where it comes from or where it is going. So it is with everyone born of the Spirit."

In the very essence of being "born again" is revival: you are being revived from your dead state to a spiritual life. That is exactly what happens to spiritually stagnating or, spiritually dead societies, communities, congregations, or churches.

5.3.   Innovation for Disruption through Revivals: Learning from the Secular World

A few years back, I was invited to give a presentation at a company retreat on culture and digital transformation. The setting was great. It was the Salvador Dali Museum[138] in St. Petersburg, Florida. There was an organization that focused on innovation for enterprises, and I was a guest speaker. What impressed me about this retreat was the vision of the CEO. It was a healthcare company, and they were going to stay in their specific vertical. However, the CEO set the tone and asked his executive team to ask the hard questions:

- Who are we? Why should we exist? What is our purpose?
- What should we focus on?

---

[138] https://thedali.org/

He was not afraid to question the existential and hard questions. Going back to the basics.

Many secular organizations have started well but soon forgot how to innovate and stay fresh. Some even have forgotten their focus and raison d'être. As I indicated in my book *How to Alleviate Digital Transformation Debt*,[139] transformation needs to start with culture. This culture needs servant leaders. It also needs a prioritization for decentralization and innovation. Organizations that did not see the signs either disappeared or became downsized and irrelevant. In the secular world, there are disruptions due to digital technologies, and companies that do not innovate and change with digital transformation have not survived.[140]

52 percent of companies in the Fortune 500 have either gone bankrupt, been acquired, or ceased to exist because of digital

---

[139] https://www.khoshconsulting.com/

[140] https://hbr.org/sponsored/2017/07/digital-transformation-is-racing-ahead-and-no-industry-is-immune-2#

disruption since 2000. One of the main reasons? They became stagnant, lost their innovative edge, and became complacent. Ignoring the appropriation of technological and cultural changes for innovation is called Digital Transformation debt – which is in the title of my recent technical book.

That is such an important lesson for churches and the need for revival.

We also need to be "transformed"—not digitally (though modernization through digitization always helps) but through the Holy Spirit—through revivals. We are accumulating spiritual debt. Many churches, Christian fellowships, or even individual Christians simply exist—through maintenance mode. That is such a contradiction when one realizes we are disciples of the greatest revolutionary in history—the Lord Jesus Christ.

"Maintenance" mentality contradicts the very spirit of revival through the Holy Spirit.

In a sense, that is what has happened throughout the ages of Christian history.

Our God is incredibly innovative. He is also amazingly creative and is no way limited by any human or natural restrictions. He also spurs men and women of God to be creative and innovative. The spark of revival—through its author the Holy Spirit—often uses men and women gifted with *His* creativity and innovation.

Every revival is unique and different, but they all share common elements, such as men and women who are moved by God through the Holy Spirit, and repentance that leads to rebirth and baptism of the Holy Spirit. There are often—but not always—signs and wonders, including miracles and speaking in tongues.

In my study of the history of revivals, I was pleasantly surprised to find that social justice and ministries to the poor were seamlessly woven into the DNA of revivals. In addition to learning about the innovation and creativity of the men and women of God who were inspired and used mightily by the Holy Spirit, I found that their passion for revival was paired with a passion for the oppressed and the vulnerable.

Revival is, at its core, a realization of the very purpose and goal of the Christian faith. We can learn a lot from the secular world. When creativity, vision, and innovation start to wane, companies stagnate and sometimes die. New more innovative companies start to challenge well established incumbents. In the business world, it is called "disruption."[141]

Isn't this "going bankrupt" or "being acquired by false or stagnating theologies" or "being disrupted" by alternative worldviews also true of churches and Christian organizations? Perhaps our own lives? I know many times in my own spiritual journey I got stagnated. Sometimes even while serving in a church or doing ministry. I thank God, He bothered me! Soon I realized the problem, and after extended time with the Word or spending a day or several days with the Lord, I enjoyed a mini-revival.

Revival is about disruption.

It is about creativity and innovation with the fire of the Holy Spirit. There is life—real spiritual life—in revivals. Churches and many Christians are on life-support systems. Existing. Maintaining. Going through the motions.

That is not what Christ had in mind when He gave the Great Commission to go and make disciples of all nations! He wants us to be wholehearted and passionate about our faith and message!

The essence of revival—always initiated by the Holy Spirit but using passionate men and women of God—is to get rid of the stagnation and creatively bring forth radical change: at times and in places as He sees fit. It is up to us to feel uncomfortable with the stagnation and struggle to bring forth the blessings that melt the hearts of men and women—to eventually baptize them with the Holy Spirit.

---

[141] https://www.capgemini.com/consulting/wp-content/uploads/sites/30/2017/07/digital_disruption_1.pdf

We can never be complacent. We constantly need to fan the fire of the Holy Spirit and hunger and thirst for His presence. Here is one of my favorite verses for revival:

> You, God, are my God,
>
> earnestly I seek you;
>
> I thirst for you,
>
> my whole being longs for you,
>
> in a dry and parched land
>
> where there is no water. (Psalm 63:1)

5.4. History of Revivals

Revival is an amazing topic that all Christians and Christian churches need to study. It is one of the most important Burning Bushes. The history of the Church is the history of revivals.

The Church began on the day of Pentecost:

> When the day of Pentecost came, they were all together in one place. Suddenly a sound like the blowing of a violent wind came from heaven and filled the whole house where they were sitting. They saw what seemed to be tongues of fire that separated and came to rest on each of them. All of them were filled with the Holy Spirit and began to speak in other tongues as the Spirit enabled them. (Acts 2:1–4)

They spoke in different recognizable languages as the Holy Spirit enabled them. When they accused them of being drunk, the apostle Peter stood up and preached the gospel with the conclusion:

> Therefore let all Israel be assured of this: God has made this Jesus, whom you crucified, both Lord and Messiah. (Acts 2:36)

There was conviction, an immediate response, and impressive results.

> When the people heard this, they were cut to the heart and said to Peter and the other apostles, "Brothers, what shall we do?"
>
> Peter replied, "Repent and be baptized, every one of you, in the name of Jesus Christ for the forgiveness of your sins. And you will receive the gift of the Holy Spirit. The promise is for you and your children and for all who are far off—for all whom the Lord our God will call."
>
> With many other words he warned them; and he pleaded with them, "Save yourselves from this corrupt generation." Those who accepted his message were baptized, and about three thousand were added to their number that day. (Acts 2:37–41)

This was the first revival, and the rest, as they say, is history.

There are so many historical revival events—all unique, all amazing—that have brought the light of the gospel to millions. But the essential elements of working with the Holy Spirit are people being convicted and "cut to the heart" and then conversions—sometimes in the thousands, hundreds of thousands, and even millions. In some revivals the revival is accompanied with speaking in tongues and miracles. As noted above, repentance is the key—we need to realize we need Christ, the Savior!

It is impossible to go through all the revivals in this book. We shall highlight some. There are wonderful publications, websites, and videos on the history of revivals. We shall reference them throughout this chapter.

Despite the incredible personal and corporate sins humanity has committed, the Lord has initiated revivals throughout the centuries. We should always remember and give thanks for His glorious works.

He wants us to respond with conviction, yet He decides when and how and by whom revivals start. Revivals—like fire—also die down over time. He also decides how long they should last.

Revivals often involve a partnership between men or women who have a burden—also prompted by the Holy Spirit—and God. Sometimes there are years and even decades of fasting and prayer prior to revivals.

Sometimes revivals give birth to other movements for the kingdom. Revivals are often associated with men and women of God who have often impacted thousands, if not millions—even after they left us to be with the Lord.

Here are a few examples throughout the ages and on different continents:

- Saint Gregory the Illuminator: 257–331 (Armenia)
- Saint Patrick: 387–461 (Ireland)
- Saint Columba: 521–497 (from Ireland but preached and spread the gospel to Scotland)
- Saint Francis of Assisi: 1181–1226
- Joan of Arc: 1412–1431
- Saint Teresa of Avila: 1515–1582
- Martin Luther—Protestant Reformation: 1483–1546
- Sadu Sundar Singh: 1889–1929(?)

5.4.1.   *British and American Revivals*

The history of the American revivals begins with what are known as the First and Second Awakenings. There were several heroes of faith who were revivalists par excellence, such as the Wesley brothers and George Whitefield for the First Awakening. There were other ordained men and women of God who were used mightily during this amazing time.

One of them was Jonathan Edwards, who, according to Britannica,[142] was the "greatest theologian and philosopher of British American Puritanism, stimulator of the religious revival known as the 'Great Awakening,' and one of the forerunners of the age of Protestant missionary expansion in the 19th century." I like Jonathan Edwards because he is an example of also superb academics, intellect and theology.

Here is how *God's Generals: Volume 3*[143] describes him:

> Jonathan Edwards is the most complex—and therefore the most misunderstood—of all the revivalists. Born the same year as John Wesley, Edwards was the son of a Puritan minister and almost considered nobility in colonial New England—though their accommodations were closer to the forts and garrisons of the Wild West than the Wesleys' peaceful parsonage in Epworth. While Jonathan Edwards would become a pastor and revivalist at the center of the Great Awakening in America, he was also an intellectual who cut his teeth on Enlightenment thought and the writings of such men as John Locke and Isaac Newton.

The Wesley brothers were also instrumental in the First Great Awakening:

> England was growing as ripe for revolution as France; yet the revolution in the British Isles would be very different. England's would be a revival called "Methodism," inspired predominantly by John and Charles Wesley. As one historian put it, Methodism and the French Revolution are the two most tremendous phenomena of the [eighteenth] century. [John] Wesley swept the dead air with an irresistible cleansing ozone. To thousands of men and women his preaching and gospel revealed a new heaven and a new earth; it brought

---

[142] https://www.britannica.com/biography/Jonathan-Edwards

[143] https://www.amazon.com/Gods-Generals-Revivalists-Roberts-Liardon/dp/1603740252/

religion into soulless lives and reconstituted it as a comforter, an inspiration, and a judge. No one was too poor, too humble, too degraded to be born again and share in the privilege of divine grace, to serve the one Master, Christ, and to attain to the blessed fruition of God's peace.

The vast network of Methodist Societies established by the Wesley brothers brought desperately needed assurances of God's mercy and love in this time of uncertainty, economic hardship, and short life expectancy. These "home groups"—what many today might call "cell groups"—orchestrated by the Wesleys provided ongoing instruction, prayer, accountability, and the necessary discipleship and fellowship that are the foundation of spiritual growth. Most importantly, John and Charles Wesley brought the message of "free grace" directly to the masses. Their greatest audience was the "contrite and lowly of spirit," who gladly opened their hearts to God's abundant provision of grace.

Perhaps the most impactful revivalist in the First Great Awakening was an amazing man of God—George Whitefield. He was a contemporary of two other giants of the First Awakening (eighteenth century to 1739 and on), the Wesley brothers. There are many books and articles written about Whitefield—always inspired. He had a lasting impact on the United Kingdom and the United States, which was a colony of the United Kingdom at that time. Here is an example of the creativity and innovation of this amazing man of God from *God's Generals: Volume 3*:

George Whitefield was known as the Great Orator, the Divine Dramatist, and the Heavenly Comet. He appealed to the emotions and used all of his faculties to bring the message of the "new birth" home to the hearts of his hearers. He undoubtedly adopted this term from John Wesley, who was probably the first to use it to refer to becoming a Christian by being "born again." This idea is taken from Jesus' statement in John 3:3: "Verily, verily, I say unto thee, Except a man be born again, he cannot see the kingdom of God." Though Whitefield incurred criticism for his theatrics, his heart was sincere and upright before God. His intentions were pure and his love for his hearers was genuine. Whitefield was an evangelistic pioneer. Moved with such deep compassion for the lost, he was the first to preach "out in the open" to coal miners and shipyard workers as they passed on their way to and from work, for they had no other opportunities to hear the Gospel. He carried the hope of God's redeeming grace not only to the working classes, but also to the nobility—he attended gatherings of famous lords and ladies, holding them spellbound with his dramatic messages.

The book continues to describe how Whitefield developed the open-air revival meetings:

George was ordained to the Anglican priesthood on January 14, 1739. He managed to preach to large crowds at the few remaining churches that would admit him, collecting significant financial contributions to defray construction costs for the orphan house he proposed to build in Savannah. His celebrity, as well as his charity, caught the interest of the Countess of Huntingdon, who invited him to deliver a presentation to a gathering of her aristocratic friends. She and several of her peers were soon counted among his most faithful supporters and patrons. It was not long before George made his way back to Bristol. Upon his arrival there, he found the clergy cold; the pulpits that had been promised him were firmly closed. But he knew from his prior experience there that the common people would not be so judgmental. Being censored by the established churches of the city, he went to the mining district of Kingswood—where there was no church at all—to preach to the coal miners "without a shepherd." He recorded his first experience preaching out in the open, of which an excerpt follows:

> I went upon a mount, and spake to as many people as came unto me. They were upwards of two hundred. Blessed be to God, I have now broken the ice; I believe I never was more acceptable to my Master than when I was standing to teach those hearers in the open fields.

George Whitefield combined his burden for the poor and destitute with his fervor to lead people to Christ. He chose a life of poverty and reaching the need of others, be that physical or spiritual. As his fame and powerful messages' impact grew, the traditional church organizations did not welcome him; he went to the open fields.[144] The churches closed. The fields opened up, and he led thousands to the Lord. The rigid four walls of churches did not limit his creativity. The important priority was to get the message out. And he did that through open-air revival meetings!

The Second Awakening went from 1800–1820s. One of the main figures of this awakening was Charles Finney:[145]

> Finney (1792–1875) was a Presbyterian minister, the leading figure in the Second Great Awakening, and a leading figure

---

[144] https://drivethruhistory.com/george-whitefield/

[145] https://tabletalkmagazine.com/article/2019/05/second-great-awakening/

in social reform. He was also an author, publishing his most popular book, *Lectures on Revivals and Religion*, in 1835.

Finney was an amazing disciple of Christ who strongly believed in the power of prayer and fasting. He also held God "accountable to His promises in the Bible." A man of faith. In many of his approaches, he used his background as an attorney in his walk with God as well as his sermons and preaching for revival.

> Charles's preaching style was markedly different from that of his contemporaries, especially because it was influenced greatly by his legal training. He did not speak down to his audiences as if he were an authority to whom they needed to conform; rather, he preached as if they were the jury deciding a case—the case being the salvation of their own souls. While other ministers criticized his common speech, use of repetition, and illustrations of everyday occupations and events, these techniques were the same tools lawyers employed to elicit a desired verdict. The members of Charles's "juries" said, "Why, anyone could preach as you do. You just talk to the people. You talk as if you were as much at home as if you sat in the parlor," and, "It seems as if Mr. Finney had taken me alone and was conversing with me face to face."394 Charles had no desire to impress or awe; he was looking for decisions for Christ and refused to deviate from that goal.

Finney also understood the Bible's teaching against slavery. The revivalists helping the poor and the needy, as well as social justice causes such as opposition to slavery, was natural and seamless.

> Upon returning to New York, Charles found that the issue of slavery had captured the consciences of many there. Those opposed to slavery included Lewis Tappan and his brother, Arthur, who had founded the New York City Antislavery Society, later the American Antislavery Society, in that same

year. Earlier, the Tappan brothers had urged Charles to allow African Americans to attend service at the Chatham Street Chapel, and he had agreed, even though whites and blacks sat in different sections. *Charles routinely denounced slavery from the pulpit, even going so far as to refuse Communion to slave owners.* (Italics added.)

There was a transition—a dying down of the impact of the First Great Awakening and then the emergence of the Second Great Awakening. Often revivals come in waves, but the duration, intensity, and frequency of these waves are completely unpredictable.

The grandson of Jonathan Edwards was also impactful in the Second Great Awakening following the legacy of his grandfather:

Timothy Dwight, the grandson of Jonathan Edwards, was installed as president of Yale University in 1795. At that time, this description was offered of Yale: "The college church was almost extinct. Most of the students were skeptical, and rowdies were plenty." Dwight had realized that Enlightenment thinking, "The Age of Reason," had influenced the students. He began holding public debates on the authority of Scripture, and he began preaching the gospel with passion. In a few years, more than one-third of the student body professed faith. The college church, which formerly had empty pews, took in new members by the dozens. Yale had only slightly more than two hundred students in those days, but these young, articulate, and passionate Christians began to make an impact. Revivals spread to other colleges in New England. Out of this came the Student Volunteer Movement, which was the beginning of foreign mission endeavors in the United States. When Dwight spoke of the revival, he called it a triumph of grace and repeatedly said, "Surely God is in this place."

5.5   Post Great Awakening Revivals

It is important to note that there is always a dying down or fizzling of the fire of revivals in the United States and elsewhere. It comes and goes in waves.

After the Second Great Awakening, there were several major revivals that impacted Christianity in the United States and, in fact, around the world.

5.5.1. *Azusa Street Revival*

One of the most amazing revivals that happened in the early twentieth century in Los Angeles was the Azusa Street Revival. The revival accelerated especially during the San Francisco earthquake of 1906, which was a wake-up call. It was also in 1906 that an African American pastor by the name of William Seymour came to minister in Los Angeles.

Here is how Wikipedia describes Seymour:[146]

> William Joseph Seymour (May 2, 1870–September 28, 1922) was an African-American holiness preacher who initiated the Azusa Street Revival, an influential event in the rise of the Pentecostal and Charismatic movements. He was the second of eight children born to emancipated slaves and raised Catholic in extreme poverty in Louisiana.
>
> Seymour was a student of the early Pentecostal minister Charles Parham, and he adopted Parham's belief that speaking in tongues was the sign of receiving the baptism in the Holy Spirit. In 1906, Seymour moved to Los Angeles, California, where he preached the Pentecostal message and sparked the Azusa Street Revival. The revival drew large crowds of believers as well as media coverage

---

[146] https://en.wikipedia.org/wiki/William_J._Seymour

that focused on the controversial religious practices as well as the racially integrated worship services, which violated the racial norms of the time. Seymour's leadership of the revival and publication of The Apostolic Faith newspaper launched him into prominence within the young Pentecostal movement.

There were amazing miracles, speaking in tongues and growth—in spirituality and numbers—that occurred in 1906. From *The Azusa Street Mission and Revival*:[147]

The Times had first covered an April 17 meeting held during the mission's first week of services. When journalists returned in mid-June, they were surprised to find how fast the mission had grown. By the Sunday evening service on June 10, less than two months after the mission's opening, reporters described the congregation as "composed of whites and blacks" numbering "several hundred people" with "scores of faces peering in from 'the windows.'" The number of worshippers would continue to rise, and by mid-July the press commonly reported regular attendance figures of five hundred to seven hundred people.

William Seymour was an African American who was blind in one eye. Yet he was one of the main leaders of this movement, and the Lord used him mightily. This is what he said about the ministry:[148]

In a short time, God began to manifest His power and soon the building could not contain the people. Now the meetings continue all day and into the night and the fire is kindling all over the city and surrounding towns. Proud, well-dressed preachers come in to "investigate." Soon their high looks

---

[147] https://www.amazon.com/Azusa-Street-Mission-Revival-Pentecostal/dp/0785216936

[148] https://www.goodreads.com/quotes/7146519-in-a-short-time-god-began-to-manifest-his-power

are replaced with wonder, then conviction comes, and very often you will find them in a short time wallowing on the dirty floor, asking God to forgive them and make them as little children.

This picture of the leadership of the movement is impressive considering it was in early 1900s and racism was pervasive in America. It shows how the Holy Spirit can melt and eradicate all racial barriers and prejudices—where saints of all races can work for His kingdom. The leader, in the center, was Seymour—a one-eyed African American—with white Americans serving with him.

Yes, there were miracles—amazing ones. But this was perhaps the greatest revival of all. The fire of the Holy Spirit does give amazing and miraculous signs and wonders. But when He fills us the racial prejudices and injustices also melts: He cleanses us and makes us holy. The lack of coverage of this amazing and historical fact by the media and Christian leaders as well as movements that are concerned by equality and social justice amazes me. The Holy Spirit is the best solution for all sicknesses, including racial prejudice!

5.5.2. Wigglesworth and Post-World War II Revivals

Smith Wigglesworth was an impactful evangelist who led many to Christ in his generation and had a lasting influence for the generations after him. Here is how a website dedicated to him describes Wigglesworth:[149]

> Smith Wigglesworth, often referred to as "the Apostle of Faith," was one of the pioneers of the Pentecostal revival that occurred a century ago.
>
> Without human refinement and education he was able to tap into the infinite resources of God to bring divine grace to multitudes.
>
> Thousands came to Christian faith in his meetings, hundreds were healed of serious illnesses and diseases as supernatural signs followed his ministry.
>
> A deep intimacy with his heavenly Father and an unquestioning faith in God's Word brought spectacular results and provided an example for all true believers of the Gospel.

---

[149] http://www.smithwigglesworth.com/

He came from a poor, hardworking family, and he was not educated. Yet the Lord used him in amazing ways. Here is one example from his ministry from the book *Smith Wigglesworth Apostle of Faith*:[150]

> When I was twenty years of age, I moved to Liverpool, and the power of God was mightily upon me. I had a great desire to help the young people. Every week I used to gather around me scores of boys and girls, barefooted, ragged, and hungry. I earned good money, but I spent all of it on food for those children. They would congregate in the sheds in the docks, and what meetings we had! Hundreds of them were saved. A friend of mine and I devoted ourselves to visiting the hospitals and also the ships. God gave me a great heart for the poor. I used to work hard and spend all I had on the poor and have nothing for myself. I fasted all day every Sunday and prayed, and I never remember seeing less than fifty souls saved by the power of God in the meetings with the children, in the hospitals, on the ships, and in the Salvation Army. These were the days of great soul awakening.

Here is another example of a mighty servant of the Lord, filled with the Holy Spirit with a great desire to help the young people: saving their souls *and* helping the poor!

He did a supernatural prophecy about coming revivals:[151]

Here is the word given by Smith Wigglesworth to Lester Sumrall in 1939.

> Smith Wigglesworth to Lester Sumrall in 1939 (WWII ready to break out) With tears rolling down his face Smith cried saying, "I probably won't see you again now. My job is almost finished." As he continued to pray he cried, "I see it, I see it!" Brother Sumrall asked, "What do you see, what do you see?"

---

[150] https://www.amazon.com/Smith-Wigglesworth-Stanley-Howard-Frodsham/dp/0882435868

[151] https://elijahanointing.org/f/word-given-by-smith-wigglesworth-to-lester-sumrall-in-1939

He said, "I see a healing revival coming right after World War II. It'll be so easy to get people healed. I see it! I see it! I won't be here for it, but you will be." And there was a healing revival right after the war.

He continued to prophesy, "I see another one, I see people of all different denominations being filled with the Holy Ghost." That was the Charismatic Revival. God raised up people during that era, like the Full Gospel Businessmen. Then Brother Wigglesworth continued, "I see another move of God. I see auditoriums full of people, coming with notebooks. There will be a wave of teaching on faith and healing." We did experience that wave he saw, and we call it the Word of Faith movement.

Then he prophesied, "After that, after the third wave," he started sobbing. "I see the last day revival that's going to usher in the precious fruit of the earth. It will be the greatest revival this world has ever seen! It's going to be a wave of the gifts of the Spirit. The ministry gifts will be flowing on this planet earth. I see hospitals being emptied out, and they will bring the sick to churches where they allow the Holy Ghost to move."

As Wigglesworth prophesized, there were waves of revivals post–World War II:[152]

After World War II, in 1947 and 1948, Pentecostals experienced two strands of an awakening, one the Latter Rain Revival and the other the Healing Revival. Large numbers of evangelicals also experienced revival resulting in many conversions. It was at this time that a great generation of Christian leaders emerged. Bill Bright began Campus Crusade for Christ. In 1949, Billy Graham's distinguished career, which popularized evangelical Christianity for a new generation,

---

[152] https://churchleaders.com/outreach-missions/outreach-missions-articles/257668-brief-history-spiritual-revival-awakening-america.html

exploded on the scene during his Los Angeles crusade sponsored by the Christian Businessmen's Committee.[30-31] An estimated 180,000,000 people attended his nearly 400 crusades, and millions more viewed on television.[32] College Revivals started as early as 1946, but when the prayer-based Wheaton College Revival of 1950 achieved national publicity, it sparked other college revivals throughout America.

Revivals also need one on one discipleship to be strengthened and established. Jesus spent most of His time disciplining the twelve and gave them the Great Commission (Matthew 28:18–20). I have mentioned this before but let me emphasize again. While ministering in Lebanon, I was discipled by The Navigators[153], which was founded in 1933 but flourished with discipleship ministries post–World War II. They were and continue to be particularly effective in the military, with college students and much more. The Navigator's ministry and revival approach is discipleship. The discipleship took the form of Bible studies, scripture memory, and discipline in learning how to grow spiritually and share the gospel. I also discipled others. Growth through discipleship is multiplicative (vs. growth through evangelistic meetings that tend to be more additive—both are important for growth). It is based on 2 Timothy 2:2:

> And the things you have heard me say in the presence of many witnesses entrust to reliable people who will also be qualified to teach others.

5.5.3. Jesus Movement

The Jesus Movement was another significant revival movement that came in 1960s and 1970s and born during the hippie generation. It was born out of the "flowers in the air" or "make love, not war" hippie

---

[153] https://www.navigators.org/about/history/

counterculture:[154] as many became disillusioned with life in Haight-Ashbury, a new set of hippie "Jesus freak" evangelists appeared in the Bay Area, urging people to follow Jesus Christ and forsake drugs and promiscuous sex. The Jesus Movement was the Christian—especially through Charismatic and Pentecostal worship—answer to the cultural revolution. Despite facing rejection from conservative Christians, the influence of the Jesus Movement can still be felt today and persists.

In the late 1970s, I came to the United States to study, and one of the Christian musicians that I loved and respected was Keith Green[155]—who was a product of the Jesus Movement. I also got involved in a charismatic church with many younger believers, especially students, who were still influenced by the Jesus Movement.

What happened to the Jesus Movement is described in *The Jesus People Movement: A Story of Spiritual Revolution among the Hippies?*[156]

> By the 1980s many JP, now several years older, had married, found jobs, entered university, or had entered into Christian ministry. Some JP dropped out on Christianity, but many settled into new JP churches or into the classical Pentecostal, Charismatic, Protestant, and Catholic churches they had attended during the heyday of the JPM. The Jesus Music had burgeoned into the CCM musical industry and had diversified and solidified its recording, marketing, and distribution channels. Some JP became more involved in the political process, and aligned with the revival in conservative politics of the early 1980s. Established JP churches like Calvary Chapel and GO continued to grow and multiply. Also during the 1980s, Larry Lea launched Church on the Rock, John Wimber the Association of Vineyard Churches,

---

[154] https://theconversation.com/jesus-people-a-movement-born-from-the-summer-of-love-82421

[155] https://en.wikipedia.org/wiki/Keith_Green

[156] https://www.christianbook.com/people-movement-spiritual-revolution-hippies-ebook/richard-bustraan/9781630873509/pd/111228EB

Wayman Mitchell went independent of the ICFG, and Larry Kreider formed Dove Christian Fellowship International (DCFI). While the JPM as a large socioreligious phenomenon had passed with the 1970s, the music and the new church networks were emerging as features that would endure through the end of the century.

Interestingly, in 2023, a quite compelling movie was made depicting the revival that started with hippies who were converted to Christ as the only source of meaning and truth. The movie was called appropriately *The Jesus Revolution*.[157]

In the 1970s, young Greg Laurie (Joel Courtney) is searching for all the right things in all the wrong places: until he meets Lonnie Frisbee (Jonathan Roumie), a charismatic hippie-street-preacher. Together with Pastor Chuck Smith (Kelsey Grammer), they open the doors of Smith's languishing church to an unexpected revival of radical and newfound love, leading to what TIME Magazine dubbed a JESUS REVOLUTION.

What left the most impression on me was the confirmation that the message of salvation through Jesus Christ and His

---

[157] https://jesusrevolution.movie/

ministry of love was "new" and "different." Isn't it amazing that the previous generations could not recognize real Christianity? The renewed discovery of the core message of our Lord and the movements of Spiritual fire melting the frozen traditional institutions has been happening throughout the ages. Nominal "Christians" and Churches on life support need to be continuously revived! It is also true of our own spiritual journeys that often become routine and cold!

Reflecting the beauty the Jesus Freaks brought to America—perhaps the greatest of young generation's revival - here are the lyrics of "Oh Lord, You're Beautiful":

Oh, Lord, You're beautiful

Your face is all I seek

For when Your eyes are on this child

Your grace abounds to me
Oh, Lord, You're beautiful
Your face is all I seek
For when Your eyes are on this child
Your grace abounds to me

I wanna to take Your word and shine it all around
But first help me to just to live it, Lord
And when I'm doing well
Help me to never seek a crown
For my reward is giving glory to You

Oh, Lord, please light the fire
That once burnt bright and clear
Replace the lamp of my first love
That burns with holy fear
I wanna take Your word
And shine it all around
But first, help me just to live it, Lord
And when I'm doing well
Help me to never seek a crown
For my reward is giving glory to You

Oh, Lord, You're beautiful
Your face is all I seek
For when Your eyes are on this child
Your grace abounds to me
Oh Lord, You're beautiful
Your face is all I seek
For when Your eyes are on.

The Jesus Movement (yes, a revolution) was amazing! There are now hundreds, if not thousands, of congregations and churches that were established as a spiritual fruit of this movement instigated by the younger hippie or rebellious generation.

And then it happened again, but this time through a university in Kentucky!

5.5.4. *Asbury Revival—February 2023*

As I was writing this book, an amazing revival started on February 8, 2023, at Asbury University in Kentucky. It started with a simple chapel service. But it never ended. It was not an organized, scheduled event. It included repentance (always a precursor to revivals) and prayer with worship. Then more worship for hours on end. Many attendees indicated they could feel the presence of the Holy Spirit. There were casting out of demons. Here is how the president of the university describes it:[158]

> On February 8, 2023, Asbury University's regularly scheduled chapel service never ended. What we have experienced

---

[158] https://www.asbury.edu/outpouring/

since that Wednesday morning has been a current of immeasurable goodness flooding our community and quickly moving into other regions of the world. Words fail any effort to communicate the abundance of experiences and stories that will leave us forever changed.

Asbury has had its share of revivals over the years. On its webpage, the university lists several revivals,[159] starting in 1905. What got mentioned most often in the news was the 1970s revival. From *Kentucky Today*:[160]

Time will tell if the revival unfolding on the campus of Asbury University will have the impact of one from 1970. The comparisons, though, are uncanny.

They both broke out during a time of unrest in America and in a normal campus chapel service. They included confession, repentance and testimonies of hundreds of students who gathered at the altar on the first day. Today, the worshiping has not stopped and has begun to spread like wildfire not only on the Asbury campus but throughout the country and even the world, thanks to social media.

Students from universities near and far have been drawn to the Asbury University campus to crowd their way into the chapel while others are watching live feeds to catch a glimpse of what is happening.

It even made the national news. Here are some of the comments by Fox News' Tucker Carlson:[161]

A growing number of people are starting to grapple with the concept of death and the spiritual life. This was once

---

[159] https://www.asbury.edu/academics/resources/library/archives/history/revivals/

[160] https://www.kentuckytoday.com/baptist_life/all-eyes-focus-on-another-asbury-revival/article_6994621a-a9b0-11ed-9cf7-67c841f9b6a3.html

[161] https://www.youtube.com/watch?v=dmuHTBo4sOc

a topic that was rarely discussed in the public sphere, but the recent phenomena of Asbury University in Wilmore, Kentucky is a sign that people are becoming increasingly interested in this topic. The university began hosting a prayer service a week ago and since then, people from all around the world have kept showing up, resulting in the university having to set up overflow chapels to accommodate the demand.

This is how the student body president, Allison Perfater, described it:

At Asbury University, three mornings a week we come together to sing praise and hear a message from a speaker. On Wednesday, February 8th, something changed in the atmosphere and it never ended. A young army of believers have risen to claim Christianity and the faith as their own as a young, free generation and that's why people can't get enough. With hundreds of calls to the university switchboard number, friends from Brazil, Indonesia, and almost every state keep coming, especially in the midst of tragedies like what we've seen in Michigan State University and even farther back to 2020. The Holy Spirit has interceded for us here at Asbury and across the nation, and though we don't know how long this will continue, it's clear that something remarkable is happening.

The movement spread to other universities and cities. Is this a revival? It will be analyzed for many years to come. But remember, each revival is different. One thing is for sure: it started with repentance and worship. It was not around a particular personality or faith "hero." Students were hungry for God and a deeper relationship with Him. And the Holy Spirit moved.

Yes, it was a much-needed revival. May it continue to spread for decades to come. Lord knows we need it.

5.6. Revival Radio TV

Revival Radio TV[162] is an excellent source on revivals around the world. I am blessed repeatedly by the ministry of Dr. Gene Bailey,[163] who, in addition to *Revival Radio TV*, also hosts *FlashPoint*.[164] In fact, recently he published a book titled *Flashpoint of Revival*.[165] It's a must-read for

---

[162] https://www.revivalradiotv.com/

[163] https://genebailey.com/

[164] https://genebailey.com/pages/flashpoint

[165] https://www.amazon.com/Flashpoint-Revival-Awakening-Transformation-Nation-ebook/dp/B0981588JP

pastors, lay leaders, and in fact, all Christians. It is filled with amazing examples of how God has worked through revivals, each of which is different, throughout the ages:

> Historically, the Church has gone through waves of revival, and they have been great cycles of learning. There's always something more that we can learn about God, about ourselves, and about how to influence the world around us.

Revival—awakening and reformation (which are also covered in the book)—is needed especially when the Church feels comfortable, opposition is at a minimum, and she becomes complacent. Again from Dr. Bailey's book:

> Through many years of not facing opposition, we've been lulled to sleep. We've become content with flashy presentations and powerless messages, because we really haven't needed anything more. The truth is, for the most part we, the Church, are pretty wimpy. We get upset when our "Seven Steps to Success" don't work out in the same week that we listen to the CD set. And if we're really honest, most of us can get by day to day without needing the Bible to be very real to us. We have our health insurance, our 401(K), our comfortable home, and church is a great place to go to socialize with our friends.

As I have stated before, I come from Lebanon, and ethnically, I am Armenian. Most Armenians live in the diaspora. We have been forced out of our homelands due to genocide and oppression. For many Armenians, Europe and the United States are much-sought-after havens for safety, comfort, and prosperity. These are the same reasons why we have waves of immigrations—including illegal immigrations of migrants who are often in dismal conditions—flooding our Southern borders.

Recently, Europe is facing waves of immigrants from the Middle East (primarily due to war) and Africa (primarily due to severe draught and economic hardships). The reason I migrated to the United States was for education in a field (computer science) that is more sought-after than the one I had majored in (pure mathematics).

Yet Armenians and other minorities living under hostile and genocidal regimes have sometimes awakened. These communities witnessed revivals that have had tremendous impact within their own communities and even outside their communities. We should not generalize or seek it, but sometimes persecution strengthens the Church and brings a Spirit-filled boldness in the body of Christ. Some of the most amazing Christian movements today are happening in countries that are hostile to Christianity and where Christians are persecuted—even martyred.

5.6.1. The Armenian Revivals

On his *Revival Radio TV* channel, Dr. Bailey dedicates several episodes to the Armenian revivals. What was so surprising for me were his observations on the impact of Armenian revivals on what happened here in the United States—linking the beginnings of Christianity (Armenia was the first nation that accepted Christianity as the official religion and the nation that fought the first war for Christ). The programs linked Armenia, the Great Awakening, and the Azusa revivals. You can find the eye-opening and inspiring historic background of awakenings involving Armenia in the *Revival Radio TV* YouTube episode:[166]

The following is an amazing statement from Dr. Bailey's introduction:

> You know as we were studying all that was going on with the Azusa Street Revival, something kept coming up. We started seeing some links all the way back to revivals that had gone way before that.

---

[166] https://youtu.be/fAU4_I2S_r0

Like me, you may not have known much about the history of Armenia and just all that happened with the revival there and how its impact had in America and *all that we experienced today, really, we trace our roots all the way back to Armenia.* (Emphasis added.)

There are three historical revivals in Armenia:

- *Armenia's first Christian nation.* The AD 301 conversion of pagan Armenia to Christianity—many seeds were planted toward this blessed conversion for Armenia. Two of Christ's disciples—Thaddeus and Bartholomew—preached the gospel in Armenia in the first century. They were martyred. They are called "First Enlighteners of Armenia."[167]

- *Revivals in Western Armenia—under Ottoman oppression.* The awakenings in America facilitated missionary movements around the globe, including Armenia:

  The Great Awakening of 1730–1755 was a period of religious revival throughout the American colonies. Isaac Bird and William Goodell, two men consumed by their own spiritual awakenings, took their message to the nations, including the Ottoman Empire. Their goal was simply to help a few, not to

---

[167] https://armenianprelacy.org/2022/11/30/saints-thaddeus-and-bartholomew/

change the nations, by introducing them to Jesus Christ. In Constantinople, the center of Muslim world, Harris Gray Otis Dwight founded the mission of American Board to Armenia and Turkey, with the same goal of introducing people to Jesus Christ. The revival was about to sweep the nation, and it changed the spiritual landscape of America forever.

- *Revivals in Eastern Armenia—under Russian occupation:*

On the Russian side of the Empire, the Christians there were coming out of the Orthodox Russian Church and there was a group there called the Molokans. The Molokan actually translated as milk-drinker and the reason they were called Molokans or milk drinkers was because they refused during the fast to not drink the milk.

They decided to hold fast to what their beliefs and they got named the Molokans. So they were pursuing God at the same time you have that sect, you've got the sect known as everything that is going on in that whole area and he is trying to find out what is happening. Now, there is a marked difference between the two empires, between . . . one side the East and the West. One side the part where Goodell and Bird were pursuing God, it took them a little bit harder to get some things—in fact they labored there for 40 years and they saw great things happening but it took a little bit longer than it did on the Russian side.

They saw a great revival happen in really in about a year.

They started seeing huge things happen. In fact, the Russian revival reached 100,000 souls very quickly. Quickly meaning within about a year, they were already at a place of seeing God move in a magnificent way and this gospel of Jesus Christ that these men took was taken on a new place in a new level in a country that no one expected. Under the Ottoman Empire, persecuted Armenians petitioned the Tsar of Russia for a safe village they could call home. Meanwhile, among the new believers from the Russian Revival were Molokans and a new group named Jumpers so called because of their exuberant noisy worship. Huge miracles followed the Jumpers and the religious began to persecute these Jumpers. Tsar Nicholas the second of Russia did not want more trouble. He was already dealing with the struggle of a faltering empire. To simplify his life, he created an edict to get the new Pentecostal so called troublemakers moved out of Russia. The perfect place to send them was to the uncertain borders of a newly conquered Eastern Armenia. Karakala, a former Russian military base, becomes a haven for these families of believers. The Tsar is happy to have both Molokans and Jumpers living so far away and the town quickly fills up. The Russian Revival of 1833 brings more incoming Russians who will carry this revival to Karakala. Among those who witness this new move of the Spirit is the Demos Shakarian family. When you talk about the Armenian revival, when you talk about the massacre that happened, the genocide and the whole story that went through all of Armenia, no matter where you start, you are going to end up at some point and you are going to hear about Demos Shakarian.

In the second YouTube video, Dr. Bailey interviews Cyntia Shakarian, the granddaughter of Demos Shahakrian. She has written a book that captures the Shaharian story appropriately called *The Shakarian Legacy.*[168]

---

[168] https://www.amazon.com/Shakarian-Legacy-Humble-Dairyman-Inspired/dp/0999455117

Kara Kala's best-known resident was named Efim Gerasemovitch Klubniken. I was unable to pronounce his name as a little girl, or even now. Fortunately, he was known as "the Boy Prophet." The first of several prophetic events which would profoundly impact my family's history happened around 1852. The Boy Prophet and his family were from Russia and settled in Kara Kala.

His family was poor, and he was considered illiterate. He had never seen a map, and he did not know anything about geography. All of which, made his abilities even more supernatural! Very early in his life, he recognized the voice of the Lord and spent much time in prayer. It did not take long for news to spread throughout Kara Kala about his extended prayer vigils and his unusual commitment to hearing from the Lord. He was known to go on long fasts as his hours of prayer expanded to several days.

At the age of eleven, this Boy Prophet had a vision as he was praying and fasting for many days in his families little house. This vision came in the form of shapes he had never seen before and could not decipher, though he recognized their importance. As he sat at the family dinner table, he began to draw what he had seen in his visions. This painstaking process lasted a full seven days. During this time he neither ate nor slept while he continued to draw, which later would be recognized as charts and maps. When the Boy Prophet's vision was complete, his parents took the drawings into the village to find someone who could interpret them. When a few people in Kara Kala saw what he had drawn, they could not believe their eyes. Everything he had written was in Russian! As each word was read, the message became clear. It was a warning from God with instructions for the citizens of Kara Kala about an event which would happen in the future.

That "event" was the Armenian genocide!
Many heeded the prophecy and migrated to the United States West Coast–Los Angeles. And then the amazing happened. In 1906,

Demos Shakarian, grandfather of the founder of the Full Gospel Businessmen's Association,[169] and his brother-in-law were walking down San Pedro Street and heard sounds of praying, singing, and speaking in tongues coming from the Azusa Street Mission, which reminded them of their own practices. This led Demos to believe that "God was also beginning to move in America just as He had in their homeland of Armenia and in Russia" and embrace the mission as a place his family could worship.

Here is how Cynthia describes it:

> Something amazing happened one day as my great-great-grandfather and his brother-in-law, good ol' Uncle Magardich Mushegan, searched for work at the local horse stables. As they walked down the streets of Los Angeles passing Azusa Street, a sound penetrated through all the noise of this busy street where day-laborers gathered to find work. The sound was so powerful it stopped them in their tracks. It was something they had heard before in Armenia. It was the beautiful sound of people praising and worshiping God by speaking in tongues. It was a miracle! They had no knowledge of anyone in this new nation who worshiped as they did back in Armenia, praising God in the Spirit!

> Later, Great-great-grandfather and Magardich said goodbye to their new friends on Azusa Street and headed back home. They returned to their families with exciting news to share about their friends in the converted horse stable. With their families, they celebrated the discovery of this beautiful presence on Azusa Street and saw it as a sign from God.

> This area would become known as the famous "Azusa Street Revival." It was here, the power of God became real to a huge

---

[169] In the next chapter, we describe the impact of Demos Shakarian, the grandson of the Demos who attended the Azusa revival on many American evangelists and American Christianity as a whole.

cross-section of races and religions. This experience marked for my family and many others, the kindling of an even larger outpouring of the Holy Spirit which would spread around the world.

The seeds were planted, and it was Demos, the grandchild of Demos who would carry the torch of faith and revival. He would have a tremendous impact on Christians in the United States and around the world, working for the kingdom behind the scenes. We shall expand more on the ministry of Demos Shakarian and the impact he had on America and the rest of world in the next chapter on the Burning Bushes of the supernatural.

The impacts and revivals came during war and persecutions of the worst kind. We know many are accepting Christ in difficult countries where there is persecution. There are revivals happening in the most difficult and oppressive countries of the world.

In closed and oppressive countries, it is the blood of the martyrs that waters the seeds of revival.

One such country is Iran.[170]

> "About 20 years ago, the number of Christian converts from a Muslim background was between 5,000 and 10,000 people," Crabtree said. "Today that's between 800,000 to 1 million people. That's massive growth." According to Operation World, Iran has the fastest-growing evangelical movement in the world.

But there was a price that was paid—and continued to be paid—that the world knows little about. The next section describes the testimony of a martyr who paved the wave to Iranian conversions.

---

[170] https://www.thegospelcoalition.org/article/meet-the-worlds-fastest-growing-evangelical-movement/

5.7.   Martyrdom and Revival: Haik Hovsepian

Christendom in Europe is dying, if not dead. Though as not as bad in Europe, America churches are not faring better. Many churches are shutting down, and there is lukewarmness that has spread. The joy is missing. Pastors are frustrated and leaving their call in droves. It saddens me to see how so many church fiefdoms will little or no spirit of unity and a vision of *the united body of* Christ.

One of those amazing stories of sacrifice and martyrdom is that of Haik Hovsepian.[171] There is actually an excellent documentary of his life, ministry, and martyrdom. Here is the synopsis:

An Islamic judge in north of Iran condemned a zealous Christian convert, Mehdi Dibaj, from Islam to death. His crime was apostasy. Dibaj had already served ten years in prison.

---

[171] https://en.wikipedia.org/wiki/Haik_Hovsepian_Mehr

> Haik Hovsepian, the leader of Evangelical Christians of Iran, chose to speak out and launch an international campaign for Dibaj's sentence to be overturned.
>
> Haik's campaign was successful, and Dibaj was released only a few days before his execution date. But, there was a price to pay. . .
>
> On January19,1994, Bishop Haik Hovsepian disappeared. Twelve days later his corpse was identified by his son. The body had been stabbed 26 times.
>
> He was not the last to be martyred. Since then several other Christians have been brutally tortured and put to death.

I am a close friend of Gilbert Hovsepian, one of the sons of Haik Hovsepian. Gilbert Hovsepian reportedly experienced persecution but later immigrated to the United States, where he chose to engage in Christian ministry among Iranian Muslim communities. He founded Send Me Out ministries:[172]

> Gilbert was born and raised in Iran in a persecuted family and church community. In the midst of the persecution, he witnessed God's power in action as he saw many Muslims come to Christ through his father's evangelism. Gilbert lost his father, Rev. Haik Hovsepian, when Gilbert was 17. His father was kidnapped and brutally martyred, having been stabbed to death 26 times.
>
> The persecution continued even after the martyrdom, which caused Gilbert to seek God's face even more. During those desperate times, Gilbert went through the 6 steps mentioned below and "Send Me Out" became his prayer and calling which later turned into a song and a ministry.

---

[172] https://sendmeout.org/about/

One of the songs in a CD with the same title as his ministry is on forgiveness. Gilbert travels regularly and leads Iranian Muslims to Christ. What a testimony of how to love our enemies and bless those who persecute us!

We do not know how God uses the impact of persecutions and martyrdoms to bring about awakenings and revivals. In eternity we will find out how the lives of martyrs and shed blood of believers impacted the Church.

One thing is for sure.

It did, and it does.

That is how the Church started. What turned the world upside down was the joyful martyrdom of the early Christian believers—from Stephen down to the hundreds and thousands who were martyred for him. The revivals and conversions of Iranians continues:[173]

> Christianity is growing faster in Iran than anywhere else in the world, according to Christian Broadcast Network (CBN).
>
> There is an incredible revival happening in this country of unrest as roughly 3,000 Muslims a month have turned away from their religion and chosen Christianity since the pandemic started back in March.

5.8.   Revival Recommendations

The author, initiator, implementer, and even finisher of revivals is the Holy Spirit. But He uses people, men and women of God who are obedient to His promptings and are willing to carry out His mission.

Evan Roberts prayed twelve years for revival! And it came!

The author of revivals is our innovative and creative God. Each revival is different. It occurs at a particular time and place. Every nation goes through periods of revivals. We should study and respect the revivals in the United Kingdom and America. But there are also

---

[173] https://chvnradio.com/articles/revival-in-iran-as-thousands-accept-jesus-christ-since-pandemic

equally impressive—sometimes even more impressive—revivals that have occurred in other places in the world.

- *Prayer and fasting.* Throughout the ages, revivals have come only as a result of intense and fervent prayer. Do you want revival in your life, in your family, in your church, and in your nation? Be on your knees. Prayer and fasting are the precursors of revivals. I am always inspired by the books and writings of E. M. Bounds on prayer. Here is what he says on prayer and revival from *Purpose in Prayer:*[174]

  > God and man unite for the task, the response of the divine being invariably in proportion to the desire and the effort of the human. This cooperation, then, being necessary, what is the duty which we, as coworkers with God, require to undertake? First of all, and most important of all—the point which we desire particularly to emphasize—we must give ourselves to prayer. "Revivals," as Dr. J. Wilbur Chapman reminds us, "are born in prayer. When Wesley prayed, England was revived; when Knox prayed, Scotland was refreshed; when the Sunday School teachers of Tannybrook prayed, 11,000 young people were added to the church in a year. Whole nights of prayer have always been succeeded by whole days of soul-winning."

- *Melting of egos—tender and responsive hearts.* Human egos and lack of forgiveness are hindrances to revival. Often revivals are accompanied and even commenced by believers being convicted of their sin, including the sin of personal grievances. We need to forgive—repeatedly. God wants us to have thick skins but tender hearts. I often go through all the people who have wronged me and forgive them and make sure I do not hold a grudge or bitterness. We cannot control

---

[174] https://www.amazon.com/dp/1641232722/ref=sspa_dk_detail_5

what others say or think about us. But we can, through the help of the Holy Spirit, control our thoughts. Once we are focused on Him in our thoughts, it influences our emotions and then our will: the boldness and actions that follow. Let heaven fill your thoughts, set your mind on things above (Colossians 3). Then you will realize how petty are the small grievances we have toward each other. Revival needs tender, forgiving, and heavenly focused hearts.

- *Think big—start small.* Revivals have typically had humble beginnings. As noted above, each revival is different. Sometimes they have started with prayers of saints who have been burdened by stagnation of spiritually—including "dead" churches—through the promptings of the Holy Spirit. Sometimes persecutions, even martyrdom, was involved. But invariably, the small and humble blessings have brought about showers of blessings! We have an example of this in the Bible: When Elijah sent his servant repeatedly if there were clouds in the sky in 2 Kings 18:44, we read, "The seventh time the servant reported, 'A cloud as small as a man's hand is rising from the sea.'" So Elijah said, "Go and tell Ahab, 'Hitch up your chariot and go down before the rain stops you.'" Elijah was thinking and believing big: impressive showers. Yet it starts with a small cloud.

- *Apply the best innovation techniques.* Revivalists are innovators. By its very nature revivals go against the culture and traditions. They shake things up in creative and innovative ways. There are known innovation techniques that are applicable to revivals. There are several. For instance, Blue Ocean is an innovative approach to create new models in the business world for disruptions.[175] It can also be applied

---

[175] https://www.blueoceanstrategy.com/what-is-blue-ocean-strategy/

to Christian organizations and churches—as it has.[176] There are others such as Design Thinking[177] techniques that can be used to generate creative ideas and test them quickly. Of course, in a Christian context, the creativity is a partnership between the revivalists and the instigator of the revival: the Holy Spirit.

- *Keep the zeal; persist and never give up.* There is a famous quote by Emerson that is spot-on: "Nothing great was ever achieved without enthusiasm." The zeal of the Lord for revival should consume us, and we should never give up. Another mantra that is key is "Fail fast and a succeed faster." It is the whole area of patiently waiting and persisting while never losing the zeal and enthusiasm. Yes, easier said than done. Like Moses or David, sometimes we will just be preparing and planting the seed for the subsequent generation to reap the harvest: get to the revival "promised land."

---

[176] https://www.blueoceanfaith.org/

[177] https://cognitiveworld.com/articles/2020/11/1/6-design-thinking-innovation-digital-transformation-debts-post-covid-19

6. The Burning Bush of the Supernatural

As we saw in the previous chapter, the Church was born at Pentecost as described in Acts 2:1–4 through the work of the Holy Spirit that the Lord had promised.

However, there has been a stagnation in Christianity and especially in mainline Western churches when it comes to the supernatural gifts and manifestation:[178]

> In the Western church, many people do not seek a manifestation of God's supernatural revelation or His supernatural works. Some people are indifferent toward the idea of experiencing the power of God's Spirit, while others reject the legitimacy of the idea outright. Many believers simply want to hear God's Word preached and to practice certain customs and traditions associated with going to church, so that they may remain comfortable and entertained. They don't really want the manifest presence of God in their midst, and they don't want to make the necessary personal sacrifice of dying to their sinful nature in order to grow closer to God.

When I became a born-again Christian and accepted Christ as my Lord and Savior, what I was—as the title of C. S. Lewis's book so elegantly describes—*Surprised by Joy*.[179] Many things in my life changed, including my countenance and my behavior. Interestingly, it included victory on *some*, but not all my bad habits. Some took years to overcome. Yet I grew tremendously hungry for the Word of God, and out of my heart flew rivers of living water (John 7:38). The reason I am sharing briefly my "supernatural" regeneration experience is to emphasize the most important miracle of all: when a person accepts Christ and becomes a new creature. The old goes away, and everything becomes new. Yes,

---

[178] https://www.amazon.com/Supernatural-Transformation-Change-Your-Heart/dp/1629111953/

[179] https://www.amazon.com/Surprised-Joy-Shape-Early-Life-ebook/dp/B01EFM8NKC/ref=sr_1_1

struggles continue, temptations persist, and the Christian life on this side of eternity is composed of successions and oscillations of victory and defeat. But then when we confess our sins and repent, the joy returns. That is the greatest evidence of the supernatural, and I wanted to set the tone of what will be discussed in this chapter.

There are for sure signs and wonders, and we are living in a "natural" world, yet God can and does act in manifestations that can only be explained as miraculous. Yet they are not violations of the laws of His eternal nature or the real laws of His creation. There are more "laws" that we are continuously discovering in physics, astronomy, biology, chemistry, and other sciences. There are more dimensions we are not aware of. We, in this natural world, are restricted in the 3D+time dimensions. God knows how to interact with these additional eternal laws and His multidimensional universe. Can He suspend them? Yes, by the very nature and definition of who He is, He can! His name is *I AM*. But personally, I believe the majority, if not all, of what we consider as miraculous and supernatural are the wonderful and truly amazing beauty, economy, laws, and even rules that He set forth in the universe. The difference is that in the multidimensional supernatural universe, He can see and act in ways we cannot imagine. Some of these laws require power—He is Omnipotent. Others need knowledge—He is Omniscient. There are laws, rules, and procedures, nevertheless. When He allowed Satan to strike Job but not kill him, He did not leave it to Satan's good intentions in keeping Job alive; He was right there protecting Job. Oh, the wonder of His love, His knowledge, and His power during our suffering.

6.1.   The Church Was Born Supernaturally

The Church was born at Pentecost as described in Acts 2:1–4:

> When the day of Pentecost came, they were all together in
> one place. Suddenly a sound like the blowing of a violent
> wind came from heaven and filled the whole house where
> they were sitting. They saw what seemed to be tongues of
> fire that separated and came to rest on each of them. All of
> them were filled with the Holy Spirit and began to speak in
> other tongues as the Spirit enabled them.

Now, throughout its history, Christians have witnessed and
grappled with supernatural manifestations of signs and wonders—
similar to the ones mentioned in Acts 2 as well as the various miracles
(e.g., healings) performed by the apostles. Were these only during
the "apostolic" age? Are the various gifts that include prophecy,
healing, speaking in tongues still applicable today?

6.2.   Can There Be Healings and Miracles after the Apostles?

Christians have struggled with this question for centuries. Do
we still have healings and miracles? In his classic book *The
Ministry of Healing*,[180] the late A. J. Gordon[181] laid it out quite
interestingly:

> Have there been any miracles since the days of the Apostles?
> To this question the common answer has been, in our times
> at least, a decided no. A call recently put forth in one of our
> religious journals, asking the opinion of ministers, teachers,
> and theological professors on this point was very largely
> answered; and the respondents were well-nigh unanimous
> in the opinion that the age of miracles passed away with the
> apostolic period.

---

[180] https://www.amazon.com/Ministry-Healing-J-Gordon-ebook/dp/B076H8XHQJ/ref=sr_1_4

[181] https://en.wikipedia.org/wiki/Adoniram_Judson_Gordon

That question and survey happened in late nineteenth century. The position of most conventional evangelical and protestant denomination is probably the same in the twenty-first century. For sure, there are especially Charismatic and Pentecostal churches that operate with the supernatural, but by and large, the age of miracles, healing, and even the manifestations of "speaking in tongues"—though all necessary for the establishment of the Church initially—are no longer mentioned or relevant in mainline Evangelical churches.

Rev. Gordon does an excellent job tracing the rational and biblical basis of miracles occurring throughout the centuries. He provides an excellent perspective rooted in the character of God who loves us and wants to heal us:

> "Every plant which my heavenly Father has not planted shall be rooted up." Sin, sickness, and death are contrary to God; they are not plants of His planting, but tares which the enemy has sown in His field.

Rev. Gordon concludes it with a powerful crescendo:

> Christ comes to the sinner, helpless, guilty, lost, and saves him just as He finds him. And so with the sufferer, when he lies "stripped of his raiment, wounded, and half dead." As the good Samaritan "came where he was and bound up his wounds, pouring in oil and wine," so Jesus will take the patient just where he is, if He takes him at all. We have not to make ourselves better in order to be healed, either spiritually or physically.

> Therefore let the sufferer take courage and lift up his weary head. Oh, you unnumbered subjects of pain and bodily torture, with hands and feet which you would use so diligently and swiftly in the service of your Lord if they were only released from the fetters which bind them—oh, you countless victims of pain and disorder, who have never

consecrated either your souls or your bodies to the service of Him who made them—hear all of you that voice of Him who speaks from heaven saying, "I am the Lord that heals you."

And if the promises of God and the teachings of Scripture and the testimonies of the healed set forth in this book might throw one ray of hope or alleviation into your sick chambers, it would repay amply the pains we have taken in its preparation, and more than compensate us for any reproach we may incur for having borne witness to a doctrine of which many, as yet, can hear only with impatience and derision. And to this last word we would join a prayer which has come down to us from a very ancient liturgy:

REMEMBER, O LORD, THOSE WHO ARE DISEASED AND SICK, AND THOSE WHO ARE TROUBLED BY UNCLEAN SPIRITS; AND DO YOU, WHO ARE GOD, SPEEDILY HEAL AND DELIVER THEM.

There is a subtle sentence in this conclusion—"if He takes him."

Rev. Gordon died at the young age of fifty-nine from influenza and bronchitis.

As we shall see, while the supernatural gifts and manifestations are as relevant today as they have been throughout the centuries, the decision who gets them, why, when, and by what frequency is entirely up to the Lord. The Lord shows mercy on whom He wants to show mercy (Exodus 33:19). He is the *Lord* of the universe. Perfect, yet often incomprehensible. He is a person who thinks, creates, decides, and acts. But also remember, He is love and, at the same time, holy—completely and perfectly separate and different.

Who has the healing, the supernatural gifts, or the mercy is entirely up to Him.

We (as I often have) might find some of His decisions unjust, especially during our struggles, including for loved ones who are suffering and are not healed. I am speaking of firsthand experiences, including the loss of my soulmate. But we are very limited in our vision and understanding.

Consider this from the physical world:

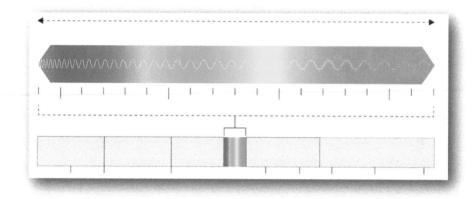

A typical, healthy human eye will respond to wavelengths from about 400nm to 750nm. Different wavelengths indicate colors in the visible spectrum ranging from violet 400nm to 750nm deep red color with a significant sensitivity peak at 555nm green. As bizarre as it may sound, there is no white or natural light "wavelength." Natural white light is a combination of different color wavelengths. Think of how light traveling through a glass prism turns into visible monochromatic colors of light called the color spectrum. Now mentally reverse the process where the same colors combine and turn into visible light where we don't discern the individual colors—even though they exist and play a role in how we feel, act, and what happens within our bodies.

What is true of our physical sight is also true of our spiritual sight. God's decision on who to heal or when to manifest the supernatural and through whom is a very complex subject.

I have—and continue to—research the supernatural. I will do so as long as I live. It is an amazing Burning Bush!

The supernatural has connections and ties to other "fringe" topics, and we shall develop these in subsequent chapters and volumes. But please remember, we can never put God "in a box" and force our preferred theology on Him. There are always layers in His Word, in His dealings with humanity, and in how and when He answers prayers. Having said that, there are also principles and laws that He has established and communicated through His Word that are rock-solid, especially when it comes to our salvation and the joy we can have here and now immaterial of our circumstances.

His answers to prayers being answered especially for supernatural miracles and manifestations is more complex. I know this firsthand. I have struggled with this personally as I prayed for the supernatural and miraculous delivery of my wife, Silva, from cancer. Others who believed in the manifestation of supernatural miracles in the twenty-first century also prayed fervent prayers.

It did not happen.

It broke and crushed me. I have never cried so much—ever![182] I felt a deep pain and emptiness. Sometimes, I still do. But also, He gave me the wisdom to seek His presence and spend extended time with Him. I got closer to Him, and He gave me a new vision and ministry. The words you are reading are the result of this new ministry.

The joy returned, though the mourning and sadness is like waves. In the beginning, it hit me very strong, and then it tapered off over time. Of course, it often comes back, especially through many photos, videos, and vivid memories. She lives in my heart forever!

We will not and cannot understand the decisions and economy of God on this side of eternity. We will struggle with it—as I have. Even the Word of God is filled with struggles and frustrations, especially in the Psalms:

> How long, O LORD? Will you forget me forever? How long will you hide your face from me? How long must I wrestle with my thoughts and every day have sorrow in my heart? (Psalm 13:1)

I remember reading a verse in Psalm 119 just before her eulogy, and it just hit me!

> I know, Lord, that your laws are righteous, and that in faithfulness you have *afflicted* me. May your unfailing love be my comfort, according to your promise to your servant. (Psalms 119:75–76)

The word *afflicted* is a very strong word. The source of the affliction is God! Afflictions can take many forms. The history of Christianity— the history of the saints—is filled with stories of struggles, sicknesses,

---

[182] The last time I cried was when I heard the news of my father passing away—that was more than forty years ago.

tortures, martyrdoms, and yes, loss of loved ones who left us too early and for no apparent reason.

Afflictions!

Yet the "affliction" is sandwiched between the righteousness and faithfulness of God and His unfailing love and comfort!

That was a divine and amazing revelation for me. Nowhere does He promise in scripture things will be easy.

We can and should expect miracles and the working of the Holy Spirit, and that is what we delve into in the next sections. Miracles—though rare and elusive—do happen today and as they have been happening throughout the ages. I like how Sid Roth puts it: "Welcome to My World where it's Naturally Supernatural."[183]

6.3.   Cessationism vs. Continuationism

There are many Christians—the majority of traditional Evangelical or Protestant congregations as well as most Orthodox and Catholic Christians—that believe the signs and wonders such as the Acts 2 are no longer applicable. They are essentially "Cessationists." Here is a clear explanation:[184]

> Cessationism is a Christian doctrine that certain spiritual gifts, as attributed to the twelve Apostles, such as miraculous signs and wonders, has ceased. These gifts were things like the Tongues we see in Acts 2, spontaneous healings and prophetic visions.

There are many divisions within the Christian body, and this is one of those topics that has divided the Church for centuries, including the twenty-first century. We shall delve deeper into Christian divisions in volume 4.

---

[183] https://www.amazon.com/Its-Supernatural-Welcome-%C2%92s-Naturally/dp/076841086X

[184] https://dividetheword.blog/2018/09/22/cessationism-the-signs-and-wonders-apostles-and-prophets-have-ceased/

The two opposing camps in this context are Cessationism vs. Continuationism.

Simply, are miracles and supernatural gifts of the Holy Spirt relevant today? Do they happen or were they a once-in-a-lifetime event that were used in what is often called the "apostolic" age— through Jesus's apostles—and ceased to be needed once the canon of the New Testament was completed and the Church established. The Cessationists believe miracles do not occur in the modern-day Church. Some of them[185] even caution us about the recent manifestations in, for instance, charismatic movements.

The Continuationists, on the other hand, believe the supernatural gifts of the Holy Spirit are relevant today. They have continued since the days of the Pentecost and do occur today in the twenty-first century.

There are different taxonomies and number of the gifts of the Holy Spirit—not to be confused with *the fruit* of the Holy Spirit. The latter should be manifested in all believers who have received Christ as their personal savior. Galatians 5:22–23 lists the fruit (singular) of the Holy Spirit:

> But the fruit of the Spirit is love, joy, peace, patience, kindness, goodness, faithfulness, gentleness, self-control; against such things there is no law.

Some of the *gifts* of the Holy Spirit (especially the *power* or *supernatural)* are listed in 1 Corinthians 12:4–11:

> There are different kinds of gifts, but the same Spirit distributes them. There are different kinds of service, but the same Lord. There are different kinds of working, but in all of them and in everyone it is the same God at work.

---

[185] See for example McArthur's book, *Strange Fire:* "The Charismatic Movement *as such* has made no contribution to biblical clarity, no contribution to interpretation, no contribution to sound doctrine."

Now to each one the manifestation of the Spirit is given for the common good. To one there is given through the Spirit a message of wisdom, to another a message of knowledge by means of the same Spirit, to another faith by the same Spirit, to another gifts of healing by that one Spirit, to another miraculous powers, to another prophecy, to another distinguishing between spirits, to another speaking in different kinds of tongues, and to still another the interpretation of tongues. All these are the work of one and the same Spirit, and he distributes them to each one, just as he determines.

According to some Christian scholars, Cessationism is on the decline. J. P. Moreland, in his book *Kingdom Triangle*,[186] states:

Cessationism is the idea that the miraculous gifts of the Spirit, such as prophecy, healing, miracles, and tongues (see 1 Cor. 12:8–10; 13:8–10), ceased with the death of the apostles and, thus, are no longer available today. Fewer and fewer Christian scholars hold to cessationism, and it may fairly be called an increasingly marginalized viewpoint. This shift in scholarly opinion has been partly responsible for the renewal of miraculous ministry in the Western church (non-Western Christians are almost never cessationist in orientation).

Throughout the centuries (from the first century till today), we have ample evidence and testimonies from reputable historic Christians recounting many supernatural signs and wonders (speaking in tongues, healing miracles, raising from the dead, and many more). So Cessationists are on very thin ice, stating supernatural manifestations have ceased after the completion of the New Testament canon and apostolic age.

---

[186] https://www.amazon.com/Kingdom-Triangle-Recover-Christian-Renovate-ebook/dp/B0BPN5Q3L9/ref=sr_1_1

6.4. The Supernatural War

We are in an incredible multifaceted and multidimensional supernatural war that has been going for millennia! Starting with the fall of mankind in the garden of Eden, the lines are drawn. Throughout his career, L. A. Marzulli,[187] who is a renowned author, filmmaker, and a great visionary who has dedicated most of his life to the study of UFOs, Nephilim, and other supernatural manifestations, consistently emphasized the importance of Genesis 3:15:

> And I will put enmity
>
> between you and the woman,
>
> and between your offspring and hers;
>
> he will crush your head,
>
> and you will strike his heel.

Here is how he describes this supernatural war between the Most Holy God and the fallen one (from *The Cosmic Chess Match*[188]):

> We know from the Genesis account that man lost his original place when he fell for the lie of the Fallen One that he would be like the Most High God. At this point, when man's authority and dominion have been usurped, we see that a provision is made to restore man to his rightful place. It is the promise of the Messiah, the One who will crush his head, which will bring about this restoration. The Most High God draws a line in the sand. He tells the Fallen One that someone will come: that someone will set things right, but the Fallen One doesn't know when. This person will come from the seed of the woman and He will defeat the Fallen One and restore the rightful place of man. In order to understand what happens

---

[187] https://lamarzulli.net/about/

[188] https://www.amazon.com/Cosmic-Chess-Match-L-Marzulli-ebook/dp/B00RN8RHXK/

> next, we need to explore where the Fallen One once dwelled, and where he dwells now and where he will eventually be cast down . . . I refer to them as dimensions. It is important for us to grasp this because it will show us why the Fallen One engages in some very desperate moves through the centuries. Understanding the concept of time and how it is perceived in the three heavens will enable us to grasp the wiles of the Fallen One and how he seeks to win the match.

This supernatural perspective and especially the war that is going on between God and the fallen one and his minions has been studied by many scholars. It is also reflected in various passages of the Bible—from the garden of Eden that led to the fall of mankind to the book of Revelation that leads to the culmination of history. It is a subject that has fascinated me ever since I was a young believer till today. I am grateful to authors and Christian leaders—often characterized as "fringe"—as well as exceptional Christian authors who have helped me to better understand the very nature of our God-created and God-imparted humanity as well as the supernatural war that has been going on for millennia.

Another one of those authors that I have come to appreciate more recently is Dr. Michael Heiser.[189] *The Unseen Realm*[190] is the title of Dr. Heiser's book, which in my opinion is a must-read for all Christians. An important theme that is developed in the *Unseen Realm* is the term *imagers*:

> The story of the Bible is about God's will for, and rule of, the realms he has created, visible and invisible, through the *imagers* he has created, human and non-human. This divine agenda is played out in both realms, in deliberate tandem. (Italics mine.)

---

[189] https://drmsh.com/ Unfortunately, Dr. Heiser left us to be with the Lord on February 20, 2023.

[190] https://www.amazon.com/Unseen-Realm-Recovering-Supernatural-Worldview/dp/1577995562/ref=sr_1_1

There is much more going on the supernatural—unseen realm—that, well, meets the eye. Job did not get it. How could he? His friends weren't much help either. In fact, Job had to offer sacrifices for them. The multidimensional, supernatural, multiheaven universe we live in is much more complex than we can imagine. We are not the only ones created in the image of God according to Dr. Heiser.

In his book *Supernatural*,[191] as well as the *Unseen Realm*, Dr. Heiser expands upon God's council—the *Elohim* (holy ones)—and the dynamics between God and these spirits. As he puts it:

> The "council of the holy ones" are real. In the first chapter of this book, I quoted a passage in which God met with his heavenly host to decide how to get rid of King Ahab. In that passage, the members of this heavenly group were called spirits. If we believe the spirit world is real and is inhabited by God and by spiritual beings he has created (such as angels), we have to admit that God's supernatural task force, described in the verses I've quoted above and many others, is also real. Otherwise, we pay mere lip service to spiritual reality.

The incident with King Ahab he refers to here is recorded in 1 Kings 22:19–23. It is a clear example that shows the dynamics between the supernatural and events in our natural world.

We need to be prepared and equipped for this supernatural war that is going on (see Ephesians 6:10–18).

The constant reminder for me is Daniel's prayer in Daniel 10, wherein his plea was indeed heard, but it required overcoming a supernatural battle: between the "Prince of Persia" (a supernatural being who had power over a locality—more on that in volume 4) and the archangel Michael. I frequently lack awareness of the underlying supernatural realm and war that permeates everything.

---

[191] https://www.amazon.com/Supernatural-Bible-Teaches-Unseen-Matters-ebook/dp/B016LT2YHA/ref=sr_1_1

Recently Jonathan Kahn wrote an interesting book highlighting that America's turning away from Christianity has caused pagan "gods" (the aforementioned imagers or Elohim) to return here to America and manifest themselves in different cultural trends. The book is called *The Return of the Gods*[192] The strangeness of the recent "woke" and "trans" culture is just one manifestation. It is a war, and it targets our children and the very souls of mankind.

6.4.1. *The Supernatural Worldview*

There are, without doubt, unusual and paranormal activities all around us. Sometimes I think the New Agers[193] are much more aware and in tune with the supernatural realm than Christians. Many paranormal and supernatural events or locations have been studied and reported. The

---

[192] https://www.amazon.com/Return-Gods-Jonathan-Cahn/dp/1636411428/ref=tmm_hrd_swatch_0

[193] I will delve into New Age in a separate chapter in volume 3. New Agers often have nefarious multidimensional and supernatural experiences (e.g., astral projections). I will also share testimonies of Christians who have come out of New Age, eye-opening to say the least!

US military and private sector interested parties have also conducted research on some of these sites.[194] We give one example below. It is a strange world out there; the supernatural is real!

Cris Putnam, who unfortunately passed away in March of 2017 at a young age (he was born in 1965—another saint who went too early but did have a lasting impact), has written one of the most significant research books on the supernatural from a Christian perspective: *The Supernatural Worldview*.[195]

To understand the paranormal and how it pertains to us as humans, it will be good to review the trilogy of man. I was glad to see Putnam quote and explain the paranormal by one of my favorite authors: Watchman Nee. Among the many books he had written my favorite is *The Spiritual Man*.[196] Here is the description of the trilogy (spirit, soul, body) of men from the *Latent Power of the Soul*[197] that extends *The Spiritual Man* with a deeper perspective on Adam's latent power:

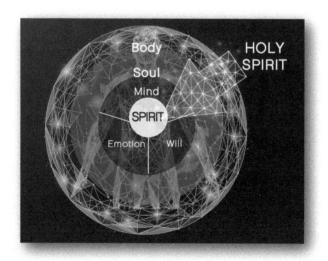

---

[194] One of the most studied is Skinwalker Ranch, https://en.wikipedia.org/wiki/Skinwalker_Ranch We shall delve deeper into it, especially in volume 3.

[195] https://www.amazon.com/Supernatural-Worldview-Examining-Paranormal-Apocalyptic-ebook/dp/B00KLG2P4M/ref=sr_1_1

[196] https://www.amazon.com/Spiritual-Man-Watchman-Nee-ebook/dp/B002S0OMOA/ref=sr_1_1

[197] https://www.amazon.com/Latent-Power-Soul-Watchman-Nee/dp/093500825X/ref=sr_1_1

"And Jehovah God formed man of the dust of the ground" (Gen. 2:7). This refers to the human body. "And breathed into his nostrils the breath of life." This describes how God gave spirit to man; it was Adam's spirit. So man's body was formed of the dust of the ground, and man's spirit was given to him by God. "And man became a living soul." After the breath of life had entered into his nostrils man became a living soul. The spirit, the soul, and the body are three separate entities. "May your spirit and soul and body be preserved entire" (1 Thess. 5:23). The spirit is God-given; the soul is a living soul; and the body is God-formed.

According to common understanding the soul is our personality. When the spirit and the body were joined, man became a living soul. The characteristic of the angels is spirit and that of the lower animals such as beasts is flesh. We humans have both spirit and body; but our characteristic is neither spirit nor body but soul. We have a living soul. Hence the Bible calls man soul.

Nee's main thesis is that when Adam fell, his powers were confined. He calls it "immobilized."

When Adam fell in the garden of Eden his power was immobilized. He had not lost this power altogether, only it was now buried within him. He had become flesh, and his flesh now enclosed tightly this marvelous power within it. Generation has succeeded generation with the result that this primordial ability of Adam has become a "latent" force in his descendants. It has turned to become a kind of "hidden" power.

Now there are religions and people who can release these powers and do unbelievable feats—"miracles." Religions around the world and throughout history have attempted to master and use this latent power—with some success. But we should be careful. This "power," which could be real and manifested through amazing feats, could be deceptive and manipulated to the detriment of our souls:

> Today in each and every person who lives on earth lies this Adamic power, though it is confined in him and is not able to freely express itself. Yet such power is in every man's soul just as it was in Adam's soul at the beginning. Since today's soul is under siege by the flesh, this power is likewise confined by the flesh. The work of the devil nowadays is to stir up man's soul and to release this latent power within it as a deception for spiritual power. The reason for my mentioning these things is to warn ourselves of the special relationship between man's soul and Satan in the last days.
>
> Yet this does not happen in Christianity alone. The Babylonians, the Arabs, the Buddhists, the Taoists, and the Hindus all try in their respective way to release the power which Adam has left to our soul. In any religion, using whatever means or ways of instruction, there stands a common principle behind all their apparent differences. This common principle is to aim at overcoming the outward flesh so as to deliver the soul power from all kinds of bondage for freer expression. Some lessons of instruction given in these religions are directed at destroying the obstruction of the body, some at uniting the body and the soul, while some are aimed at strengthening the soul through training and thus enabling it to overcome the body. Whatever the ways may be, the principle behind them all is the same. It is important to know this or else we will be deceived.

Putnam then dedicates deep analysis of all the "supernatural" and paranormal activities that have been getting special attention—as the postmodern man still attempts to fill his or her void with anything but God. He exposes *pantheistic monism* underlying many modern-day paranormal manifestations.

> Although the veridical portion is neutral, there is an emergent paranormal worldview associated with the NDE.[198] As a form of universalism, it holds that all spiritual systems flow together into one. An appropriate academic classification is pantheistic monism . . . . the pantheist reasons that the soul of every person is a piece of the same universal soul, and individuality is a pernicious illusion . . . Oneism is now arguably the dominant religious point of view in the West.

We shall be expanding upon this also in subsequent chapters—especially on New Age—contrasting Oneism and Twoism. Peter Jones[199] is an excellent source that contrasts these two fundamentally opposing worldviews.

Here are some of the topics covered in Putnam's must-read book that I highly recommend:

- *Near-Death-Experiences.* Putnam discusses the potentially deceptive nature of near-death experiences (NDEs) and suggests that the best way to understand what lies beyond death is to rely on a more credible authority such as Jesus, who authenticated his view by returning from the dead. It argues that NDEs may have a positive or negative outcome, but they should not be used to draw universalist conclusions. Jesus's teaching that no one will be convinced if someone should rise from the dead is the best advice for understanding what lies beyond death.

- *Telepathy, Dreams, and Remote Viewing.* There are plenty of examples of dreams in the Bible—the interpretation of dreams is from God (Genesis 40:8).[200] For telepathy and remote viewing, Putnam gives several examples, including

---

[198] Near-Death Experiences (NDE).

[199] https://www.ligonier.org/learn/articles/one-or-two

[200] https://faithgateway.com/blogs/christian-books/decoding-your-dreams

biblical examples. For the biblical position, he quotes from a Baptist pastor:

> Neither telepathy nor clairvoyance appears deserving of our censure. They are natural properties of the mind, and only reveal the wondrous faculties with which the Almighty has endowed us. If it is possible to send out circling waves of wireless telegraphy, which widen out as the rings from a stone cast into a pond or lake, and can only be appreciated where the receiver and the transmitter are perfectly attuned, so it is not difficult to believe that our minds are constantly radiating motions and influences through our brains, which are perceived by sympathetic correspondence with other brains.

- Satan, Demons, and the Ghost Hypothesis:

  Putnam observes:

  > The Hebrew background to Paul's discussions of rulers, powers, and principalities comes into clearer focus (Ephesians 3:10, 6:12; Colossians 1:16, 2:15). As demonstrated prior, it is most likely true that more than one sort of entity falls under the broad category of "demon." Perhaps these fallen "sons of God"—labeled little-"g" gods—are one and the same as the rulers (archons), but what about the more commonplace evil spirits (poneron pneumaton) encountered in the Gospels and Acts (Matthew 12:45; Luke 7:21, 8:2; Acts 19:12–16)? The "ghost hypothesis" may account for some of these entities.

It is not clear what *ghosts* and *daemons* are. An oft-cited theory is that *daemons* are the disembodied spirits of the Nephilim. Perhaps they are fallen angels. Another theory is that they are the spirit of the departed—human ghosts.

According to Putnam and his impressive research (with many excellent references, including Chuck Missler[201] and others):

> If we understand the term "demon" in a manner consistent with its early Greek use, as well as in later Christian developments, it could arguably be understood to encompass all evil spirits aligned with Satan. In this way, one could preserve the important distinctions made by Missler but argue that although all fallen angels are demons, not all demons are fallen angels. Of course, Missler's arguments are directed toward the controversy over the Nephilim and the identity of the 'sons of God' in Genesis 6. I have addressed that debate ad nauseum and see no need to argue it here. The Supernatural Worldview unequivocally supports that the "sons of God" are spirit entities.

In volume 4, we shall delve deeper into the Nephilim and relate it to modern-day apparitions such as UFOs as well as other manifestations (e.g., crop circles, elongated skulls, cattle mutilations, hybrids) and discoveries such as ancient civilizations and giants.

These unusual or supernatural manifestations are not disconnected and distinct. Also, they are not all nefarious. However, the battle lines that are set in Genesis 3:15 continues; fortunately, we are on the winning side!

6.5. Miracles and Miracle Workers

Signs and wonders, including miracles of healing, happen in different ways, by different people, and at different times. They have occurred throughout history. God is no respecter of denominations or backgrounds. There are charismatic Catholics who speak in

---

[201] https://en.wikipedia.org/wiki/Chuck_Missler

tongues as well as Orthodox, Pentecostals, and Protestants of any denomination whom God has imparted supernatural gifts.

But miracles, especially the healing kind, do not always happen. On this side of eternity, we will never comprehend the factors behind God's choices regarding the regularity of miracles.

The Lord knows how many times I have prayed and claimed miraculous healing for my wife, Silva, as she was deteriorating from cancer. She tried everything—natural and supernatural. It was not meant to be.

One great consolation I had was the fact that though she was weak, *she was never in pain*. She never took morphine or any other type of pain-easing medication. She went peacefully surrounded by her four sons, daughters in love, and her soulmate! For me, that was a miraculous consolation. I do not know how I would have taken it if she suffered from pain on top of it all.[202] God spared her. And me.

On her last trip to Armenia in 2018, she traveled with several ministers who had supernatural gifts. Among those were Rev. Dr.

---

[202] I know many do—we do not understand it. God is gracious.

Annie Arakelian,[203] Ken Fish,[204] and Rev. Haig Kherlopian.[205] These are anointed servants of the Lord. Ken Fish has many supernatural gifts. He recently wrote a book titled *On the Road with the Holy Spirit: A Modern-Day Diary of Signs and Wonders.*[206] Dr. Annie Arakelian also has a supernatural anointing (see below) with visions, and she uses her gifts to bring spiritual deliverance through her ministry. She is the author of *Entering Heaven's Gateways.*[207]

Why am I mentioning these? Silva was surrounded with many saints who had supernatural gifts of the Holy Spirit with special anointing. Amazing Spirit-filled believers! She herself sought impartation repeatedly. God did use her—mightily! Hundreds, if not thousands, of lives were touched through her ministry. After her passing, I was overwhelmed with the cards, e-mails, notes, calls, and letters I had about how Silva touched them and contributed to their spiritual growth—from all over the world. One thing that impressed me about Silva is that even though she and countless others prayed for a miracle, she never once blamed God. She never complained to Him. She called the devil the "loser" when her situation was difficult to bear. That, too, for me is a miracle, and I hope I can emulate her.

However, God decided not to heal her supernaturally.

Not all prayers get answered *the way we want them answered.* That sounds like a cop-out, but it is true, and frankly, I struggle with it. Oh, how I wish I understood how the supernatural works.

I am trying. I am unable to consistently resolve it .

But I know this. He is faithful, and His love endures forever!

---

[203] http://lightofthecomforter.org/

[204] https://orbisministries.org/

[205] https://www.linkedin.com/in/haig-kherlopian-a6804431/

[206] https://www.amazon.com/Road-Holy-Spirit-Modern-Day-Wonders/dp/1636412548/ref=sr_1_1

[207] https://www.amazon.com/Entering-Heavens-Gateways-Supernatural-Breakthroughs/dp/1662861117/ref=sr_1_1

6.5.1.   Examples of Modern-Day Miracles and Visions

There are plenty of examples of gifted and Spirit-filled Christians who have experienced supernatural healing miracles and who also have been used by the Lord to heal others supernaturally. The list is long. Can we vet them all? No, that is impossible! But I know some of them personally, and I can testify that their experiences are real. Praise the Lord!

Having said that, as a scientist, I am used to ask for evidence and study the facts. There are also many strong, wonderful, Spirit-filled Christians who prayed for years, but the Lord never healed them. As noted above, I also know that firsthand miracles and supernatural healing do not have a simple formula.

Simplistic answers like "just believe" or "have enough faith" are commendable but do not always work!

Having a deeper understanding of His transcendence is essential. We cannot put God in a box. In the book of Job, the entire conversation between Job and his friends did not bring up—not even once—the real culprit of Job's sufferings! There is much more going on in the supernatural realm, let alone the very nature and character of God and how He deals with us. Things are not what they seem. God is amazing. He is incomprehensible yet imminent and is looking for us to come as children and seek Him. He is holy, separate, different, above all in every way. Yet He is love and so near to us, especially those who seek Him with a pure heart. Transcendent and yet imminent. Holy and love.

The other side of the coin is to be innocent seekers yet be also wise. In other words, healthy skepticism is also important. There are several examples of "fake" prophets in the Old Testament who prophesized what the leaders wanted to hear. But equally, there are also miracle workers—as in the case of the pharaoh's magicians—who could perform miraculous feats with nefarious spiritual powers.

In the next sections, I will present some examples of anointed servants of the Lord with supernatural gifts.

6.5.2.   A Catholic Priest with the Gift of Healing

Dr. Francis Sizer is a Roman Catholic priest.[208] In his book *Power Encounters*,[209] he gives several impactful examples of miraculous healings. Here is one:

> One day I visited a 65-year-old woman named Anne who was dying with stage four cancer. During that time people, in general, with a terminal condition stayed in the hospital to die. Insurance companies didn't chase them out. Anne was put on morphine to kill the pain of the cancer. The family and staff of the hospital knew she was about to die. The smell of death filled the air in the private room. I stepped over to her, knowing the Holy Spirit was with me. I prayed over the woman by casting out the spirit of death and the spirit of cancer in Jesus' name. Her eyes grew enormously wide as the miraculous power of God went through my right hand into her body. I commanded her to get up out of bed and walk with me down the corridor. As we walked, she got visibly stronger and stronger. The nursing staff came running toward us and shouted to the woman, "What are you doing out of bed? Get back in bed now." I smiled at the woman and it put her at ease as we returned to the room. The nurse wanted to know what had happened. I told her I prayed for a miracle. She said that she would have to get the doctor. As the story unfolded, the woman's health was so drastically different that the doctors retested her and could find no cancer in her body. She was discharged a day or two later with a clean bill of health and a love for God that was stronger than ever. She was instrumental in witnessing to her miracle at my first healing service a few months later.

---

[208] From his book: "An ordained Roman Catholic priest following eight years of study. He holds three accredited master's degrees and a doctoral degree from the University of Maryland. He ministers in healing—physical, emotional, and spiritual."

[209] https://www.amazon.com/Power-Encounters-Unlocking-Supernatural-Experiences-ebook/dp/B07C193D9Q/ref=sr_1_1

> Word of the miracle spread throughout the hospital and throughout my parish. There was a buzz in the air.

6.5.3. Prescriptions and Road Maps for the Supernatural

Joshua Mills is an anointed ordained minister with many gifts. He has ministered in six continents and authored more than twenty books. In his book *Moving in Glory Realms*,[210] he shares principles, techniques, and practices—working miracles. I am also impressed by his research and medical knowledge and how he uses it for miraculous healings.

> There are many different methods of laying hands on the sick. Let the Spirit lead you. You can place your hands on the person's head, on their neck, or on the affected area. You might be led to have the person put their hand on the area of need, and then you place your hands over their hands or on their head. There is no one right way. You are anointed to work miracles. God is faithful to show you how. Be willing to listen to His still small voice in the process.
>
> When I minister to the sick, I ask God to show me how to lay hands on them. He often gives me specific instructions for doing it, depending upon the condition I'm dealing with. For instance, when praying for healing from carpal tunnel syndrome, I ask the person to stretch out the arm that bothers them. I begin working the miracle by commanding those muscles to strengthen and for the carpal tunnel area to open. Medically speaking, this issue causes pressure on the median nerve, resulting in subsequent weakness in the wrist.

He gives several examples. He has had great success in ministering this way. Hundreds have been freed from their pain and given a new

---

[210] https://www.amazon.com/Moving-Glory-Realms-Exploring-Dimensions/dp/164123086X

start. Here is one example – the testimony of Amanda, from Aukland, New Zealand :

> From that day you prayed for me I have been healed. Completely! Praise the Lord! I was under the top hand specialist here in Auckland, and that very week after I was healed I had two appointments scheduled—one with the neurologist at Auckland Hospital and the second an MRI scan at the largest hospital in New Zealand. Well, after both tests, the team of hand specialists have written a letter to my family doctor stating that there are no longer any symptoms of carpal tunnel, and they have dismissed me from the government medical system. Hallelujah!

6.5.4. Dreams, Visions, and Deliverance

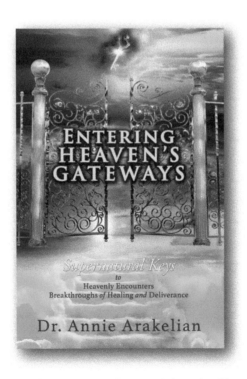

These are also unusual yet amazing spiritual gifts. Like all of you, I constantly have dreams—every day—but do not know if they are from the Lord or if I had too much pizza the night before. Some of these dreams do tend to carry some deeper spiritual meaning—due to the subject, images, and people (some of whom have passed away). So far, I have never had visions while awake or heard the voice of God. Some claim they have.

Among those who even have visions while carrying out a conversation is Dr. Rev. Annie Arakelian.[211] On her recent book *Entering Heaven's Gateways*,[212] she mentions several supernatural experiences—including hearing the voice of the Lord, dreams, and visions. Here is one example:

> Once when I was preparing a study for a women's meeting, I was very tired and drained with no energy left. I was running out of time and had no time to rest. I prayed, "Lord, I am so tired and I need rest, but you know I need to finish preparing the teaching for tonight." I heard the voice of the Lord asking me to lie down on the couch, which I would not typically do during the day but I did as the Lord asked. As soon as I lay down, I passed out and fell into a deep sleep. It was a trance-like experience. I saw myself in the heavenly realm where refreshing waters were flowing. When I woke up, I found myself jumping and giggling like a child. I was so refreshed and energized that I was sure I had been sleeping for hours but when I checked the time, only 3 minutes had passed. Right then the Lord spoke to me again, "My child, learn to tap into the supernatural resources that are yours in Christ Jesus." In visions during ministry time, I have seen Jesus carrying others to this realm in the spirit to give them rest in the refreshing still waters.

---

[211] Dr. Rev. Annie Arakelian is the founder and director of Light of the Comforter Ministries Inc. and Light of the Comforter Wholeness Haven, LLC. Her mission and vision are to "Equip, Empower, Train, and Restore the army of the Lord and release them into their calling and destiny to advance His Kingdom on earth."

[212] https://www.amazon.com/ENTERING-HEAVENS-GATEWAYS-Supernatural-Breakthroughs-ebook/dp/B0BQ51MHHS/ref=sr_1_1

In addition to serving on the board of her nonprofit, I have had many blessed conversations with my sister in the Lord. While engaging in certain conversations, she would have visions in the midst of our discussion. Additionally, she had a strong bond with my wife, Silva, who would also share with me the visions Annie experienced during their fellowship. Annie's visions of Silva after her passing away were comforting and encouraging.

This is how Annie described their ministering together in Armenia—during the last trip that Silva took there to bring hope to many:

> In 2018, we went to Armenia on a mission trip with a powerful team who joined us from different states. Up until that point, I thought I knew Silva intimately. I was wrong! We got even closer as sisters in Christ as we worked together, woke up together, and laughed together. We felt tired and exhausted from long trips to the villages and sometimes hardly slept or ate, but yet we were empowered and encouraged by each other's prayers and support. When we had no energy left, we laughed so hard and gained our strength back. It was the powerful joy of the Lord sustaining us. Our bond got stronger than ever. We became each other's support and cheerleader. During ministry, both felt the pain and demonic oppression from those who we were ministering to. Yet at the end of each night service, we would glorify God for what He did and then carried all the burdens from each other's heart to Him.

6.6. Supernatural Testimonies: Changed Lives and Impactful Ministries

Supernatural encounters changing lives are perhaps the most powerful personal testimonies demonstrating the reality of gifts and wonders operating these days. I will give my personal journey and encounters in this domain, but before that, I would like to illustrate here two examples: one from a Turkish believer from a Muslim background and the other an Armenian believer from a Pentecostal background, both of whom witnessed the supernatural and had profound evangelical impact around the world.

6.6.1. Işık Abla

A few years ago, I had the privilege of meeting Işık Abla and her husband in Cambridge, Massachusetts. I was with my wife, Silva, and in fact, she was the one who had arranged the meeting with Işık Abla. It was a blessing and honor to meet our sister and her graceful husband. This was not the first Turkish believer couple that Silva and I had fellowship with. When I was doing my thesis in Wisconsin, our closest friends were a couple where the wife was a Turkish believer (also converted from a Muslim background) with an American husband. We had many precious times in prayer and Bible study together. It is such a blessing when the Holy Spirit melts all racial and national divisions and helps us fellowship with joy.

Işık Abla's story and testimony is amazing and nothing short of miraculous. She has been very impactful, and the Lord has used her to lead many Muslims to Christ and be a powerful testimony for the Lord. She has 5.4 million followers on Facebook.[213]

She had a very difficult life and went through hardships, abuses, and two divorces (she ended up leading her second husband to the Lord). However, what is most interesting and amazing is the working of the supernatural in her life. I strongly recommend her book titled *I Dreamed Freedom*.[214]

This is how she describes her struggles, emptiness, and yearning for the Lord:

> I was very attracted to this teaching of Jesus. I wanted to comprehend it. I wanted to understand His unconditional love. I had searched for this type of love while I lived as a young adult in Turkey. I had written essays about it and spent hours thinking about it. Unfortunately, the Muslims did not comprehend unconditional love. The Turkish men I dated left me feeling unworthy of myself. I thought I had done everything right in my life, and as a result I was victimized by men. Because I was treated disrespectfully, I decided to be morally bad myself. Kara, my best friend at the time, became my worst enemy later—and perhaps she was even then. She said, "I will teach you how to be bad and how to deal with men. You will live your life like a man." She set me up with guys. She was very proud of

[213] https://www.facebook.com/isikablatv

[214] https://www.amazon.com/I-Dreamed-Freedom-Isik-Abla/dp/0985590106/ref=tmm_pap_swatch_0

that she slept with more than a hundred men. I partied with her and them and lived the lowest life possible. I was so thirsty for love, but no relationship was able to satisfy that thirst.

She encountered the Lord but had struggles and difficulties. One day she receives a call from a pastor and his wife to spend a weekend with them. You can read the details in Chapter 36[215] of the book. The supernatural incident that I would like to highlight here is the following:

> I certainly didn't expect what happened next! As soon as I entered their house, this preacher fell on his face and started praying in a different language. He was "speaking in tongues"—and everything he was saying was in perfect Turkish. He was interceding on my behalf and confessing my intimate sins and struggles with God, all of the things I had been praying to the Lord about earlier. There were other people in the room at the time. They were looking at my face, which had probably turned yellow by then. They knew something was happening, but they didn't understand completely what it was. I was the only one in the room who could understand what he was saying. Then this man of God looked me in the eye. He pointed his finger at me and said with a loud and firm voice, "Sister, I don't know what I just said, but you seemed to understand it. Take it seriously." Then he repeated himself and said, "Take it seriously. You have a high calling that I cannot describe with words. Take it seriously."

She did. The result is one of the most amazing and blessed ministries not only to the Turkish nations but to many Muslims and even Armenians—with miracles and supernatural manifestations!

---

[215] Which also includes another miracle in her driving a long distance with an empty gas tank!

For instance, she recounts the story of a Muslim mother that brought her child with advanced autism. The mother brought the child to sister Işık, and she, in turn, brought it to the attention of her pastor. And the amazing happened. After the pastor indicated it is only Jesus that heals, he prayed for the child. Here is what happened:

> Early the next morning, my phone rang at 6:30 a.m. It was the mother of the autistic child. She was screaming and crying and laughing at the same time. She said that for the first time since her daughter was born, her daughter had woken up crying and calling for her mother. We rejoiced over this miracle performed by our Lord Jesus. As I said before, I have witnessed many of Jesus's miracles among the Muslim people.

Praise the Lord!

6.6.2. Demos Shakarian

In chapter 5 I touched upon the Armenian Revivals, the Shakarians, and their impact on revivals within the United States. Many years ago, I had read the book *The Happiest People on Earth*.[216] It is an

---

[216] https://www.amazon.com/Happiest-People-Earth-personal-Shakarian/dp/1539915808/ref=tmm_pap_ swatch_0

amazing true story of the Shakarian family's journey from Armenia's Kara Kala village to Los Angeles and the many miracles that God did especially through Demos Shakarian—the founder of the Full Gospel Men's Fellowship International[217]—from their website:

> In the early 1900's . . . led by God, the Shakarian family escaped the Holocaust in Armenia and made their home in Downey, California where they started a 20-Acre dairy with three cows. Faith in God, good judgment and hard work eventually multiplied that first little herd one-thousand fold, until in 1943 the Shakarian herd had reached three thousand, the largest private dairy in the United States at that time. Their story is found in the book, "The Happiest People on Earth," read by millions of people and translated into 25 languages.
>
> In January 1953, after receiving a God-given vision the previous month (click here to read about the vision), Demos Shakarian incorporated FGBMFI, beginning with one small chapter of businessmen meeting every week in Clifton's Cafeteria in Los Angeles, California.

---

[217] https://www.fgbmfi.org/

The Demos Shakarian story is filled with testimonies of the supernatural. After a miraculous answer to prayer of a member of the congregation's mother joining her daughter from Armenia, Brother Demos recounts:

> Today the sense of expectancy was high, each one wondering what form the Lord's next blessing would take. Perhaps someone would be healed. Perhaps someone would receive guidance. . . . Even as I was thinking this a strange thing began to happen—not to someone else—but to me. As I sat there on a rear bench with the other boys, I felt something like a heavy woolen blanket settle over my shoulders. I looked around, startled, but no one had touched me. I tried to move my arms, but they met resistance, like I was pulling them through water. Suddenly my jaw began to shake as if I were shivering with cold, although the "blanket" felt warm. The muscles in the back of my throat tightened. I had a sudden yearning to tell Jesus that I loved Him, but when I opened my mouth to say so, out came words I couldn't understand. I knew they weren't Armenian, or Spanish, or English, but they poured out of me as though I'd been speaking them all my life. I turned to the boy next to me and he was all grins. "Demos's got the Spirit!" he shouted, and all over the church people turned.

Demos suffered from hearing loss. He recounts from his earlier years:

> I began to notice that I wasn't hearing as well as the other kids in the fifth grade, Mother took me to the doctor. "I can tell you what the trouble is, Zarouhi," the doctor said, "but not what to do about it. Demos has broken his nose and it's healed wrong. Both the nasal passage and the ear canals are blocked. We can try an operation, but they aren't usually too successful."

After receiving the Holy Spirit and speaking in tongues, the Lord also healed (at least 90 percent) his hearing miraculously—the supernatural at work! Here is how he recounts it, including the supernatural hearing of God's voice:

> As I lay there in my room, time took on an eternal quality. And in that eternity I heard a voice. It was one I recognized very well indeed, for I had heard it often in my green cathedral out in the cornfields. Demos, can you sit up? It asked. I tried. But it was useless. Some incredibly strong, yet infinitely gentle power held me where I was. I knew that I was a strong boy—not as strong as Aram Mushegan, but very tough indeed for a thirteen-year-old. Yet my muscles had no more strength than a newborn calf's. The voice was speaking again. Demos, will you ever doubt My power? "No, Lord Jesus." Three times the question was repeated. Three times I answered it. Then all at once the power which had been all around me seemed to be inside as well. I felt a surge of superhuman energy—as if I could float right out of the house and sail the heavens in the power of God. I felt as if I could look down on earth from God's perspective, see all human need from the vantage point of His supply. And all the while He was whispering to my heart, Demos, power is the birthright of every Christian. Accept power, Demos. And suddenly it was dawn. I could hear the mockingbirds outside my window. I sat up with a start. I could hear what? It had been years since I had heard a bird singing.

There are many testimonies of Demos Shakarian's impact on the world and the lives of many leading evangelists. He was not an evangelist himself. He encouraged, supported, and touched the lives of so many. A man of vision, he was usually working behind the curtain and supporting those who are on the forefront. Here is one of my favorites from none other than Reinhard Bonnke, the evangelist:

Demos Shakarian was a man filled with the Holy Spirit and a giant of faith. I met him the first time in South Africa, and we became instant friends. His ministry had rapidly spread all over the world, and multitudes of business people found Jesus as their Savior. I saw these branches wherever I went: Europe, Asia, Australia, Africa . . . Demos invited me to be the keynote speaker in Melbourne, Australia. I spent high-quality time with this great man of God. His life and work has blessed and inspired me to carry the burning torch of the Gospel across the whole earth!

The list that influenced the lives of many Christian leaders and believers goes on and on. Cynthia Shakarian indicates how her grandfather impacted so many well-recognized servants of the Lord—names we could readily recognize, such as Billy Graham, Oral Roberts, Dr. Charles Price, Kathryn Kuhlman, and Kenneth Hagin.

An amazing supernatural life!

6.7. Personal Testimony and Recommendations

The previous two examples are giants of faith in the twentieth and twenty-first century. There are many others. We saw how they impacted Silva and many others – sometimes through miracles and supernatural manifestations.

When I accepted Christ after an evangelistic meeting and started to get discipled by The Navigators, I developed a tremendous hunger and thirst for His Word. In addition to Bible studies and the Topical Memory System scripture memory, I went ahead and memorized other passages, including the whole letter of the book of Philippians. I was filled with joy.

These were many times of inner joys and manifestations. I also had tremendous thirst and hunger for Christian literature. I believe I read the entire works of Dr. Francis Schaeffer and many books by C. S.

Lewis as well as Christian classics from giants such as Watchman Nee, Andrew Murray, A. W. Tozer, Thomas A. Kampis, and many others.

But there was more.

One day I was walking to a prayer meeting. In the middle of my walk on the street, I had what I believe was an extra filling[218] of the Holy Spirit. I had not asked for it and, at the time, did not understand what was happening. The experience was what our Lord described in John 7:38:

> Whoever believes in me, as Scripture has said, rivers of living water will flow from within them.

It was different from anything else that I have experienced—then or now. It was bubbling, and every now and then when I spend long periods of time in prayer with a clear conscience, I have trickles of it. But nothing like that abundant filling on a street in Beirut that came so unexpectedly. Oh, how I yearn to experience it one more time, and if that is how heaven will be, I cannot wait.

There was a second supernatural experience. In the early 1980s, I was praying in my campus room and had heard—even seen— enough of Pentecostal visions and speaking of tongues that I asked the Lord *earnestly* to give me this gift. I do not understand how the impartation of Holy Spirit gifts really happens. Even though some teach on it, ultimately these are *gifts*, and it is up to the Giver to decide when and how to impart them. In any case, I did receive this gift and started to speak in tongues. From that moment on, I can speak anytime, and it is edifying for me. It is not a language that I understand, and I do not know what I am saying. But it is real. It is a prayer language for me. I do not know if this is a different language or just utterances for the Holy Spirit.

---

[218] A "baptism" of the Holy Spirit? Perhaps. There are different opinions on this, and many scholars consider we are baptized with the Holy Spirit the moment we believe. Whatever it is called, it was unique and different, and I have been seeking it since.

The supernatural is real! Every believer has the potential of receiving supernatural gifts. It is up to Him when, which, and how much to impart these gifts.

Manifestations of the supernatural are really the outpouring of revivals. The supernatural is the ultimate Burning Bush. From *Supernatural Upgrade:*[219]

> The supernatural of God is manifesting all around us, but we must be sensitive enough to notice it. Like Moses, we must go, see, and look! We must answer when He calls us, "Here I am!" When we perceive heavenly activity and respond, godly supernatural encounters happen.
>
> When Moses went over to see the burning bush and hear what God had to say, He told Moses His plans for His people and how Moses would play a part in those plans. Each sign and wonder that shook Egypt was told to Moses beforehand. Though Moses had received the impartation by being in the presence of God, he had to learn how to trust in the power and the presence of God.

The hunger to seek His glory ("Let me go and see") and the readiness to respond ("Here I am, Lord) go hand in hand. They are the precursors to supernatural manifestations.

So what are the pragmatic recommendations for this last chapter on the Burning Bush of the supernatural:

a. *Gifts of the Holy Spirit have been real and present throughout the history of the Church.* Even though you might not have seen or experienced them, they are nevertheless real and available *now*. There is absolutely no teaching in the Word that indicates they would have stopped at some junction—either the completion of the canon of scripture or the end of the apostolic age. Those are

---

[219] https://www.amazon.com/Supernatural-Upgrade-Walking-Glory-Realm/dp/0768462304/ref=tmm_pap_swatch_0

human assumptions. Though not manifested as frequently and readily as we like, the gifts are real—even in this age!

b. *Be wary of fake and even demonic manifestations—test the spirits.* There are two additional major sources of supernatural manifestations: fake manifestations and "signs and wonders" instigated by the enemy. Both are dangerous and should be tested, rebuked, and avoided. What appears as a supernatural manifestation does not immediately imply it is from the Holy Spirit. There are many documented cases of fake miracles. Humans have latent power of their souls. There are also documented cases of demonic manifestations. In every case, the gifts of the Holy Spirit always confirm the Word of God and never contradict it. Remember, the greatest supernatural gift is the salvation of our spirits – when the Holy Spirit comes and dwells in us. We are and continue to be sinners and subject to failings this side of eternity.

c. *Seek the gifts.* Pray to the Lord to give you the gifts. It happened to me. But there are others who have sought the gift of speaking in tongues, but the Lord decided not to give it to them. Silva was one of those. The Lord had given her other gifts not mentioned in 1 Corinthians 12. Oh, how I wish I had her gifts. It is entirely up to Him who gets what and how much. Remember, it is a *gift*. None of us deserve it, and we should be content and grateful to whatever gifts and abilities He has given us. We need to take our talents and use them for His glory. Nevertheless, it does not hurt to ask for additional supernatural gifts, and we are encouraged to do so. So ask!

d. *Do not be prideful or arrogant.* Even Satan is anointed. But he uses it for rebellion and destruction. There are many examples of servants of the Lord who have started well with many gifts and ended up being a disgrace to the kingdom. You should stay humble and always remember your gifts *and* anointing are from Him. He (the Holy Spirit) decides who gets it. He decides what gifts are imparted on whom. He decides how much. Always focus on that, and stay humble.

e. *Let the Word of God dwell in you richly.* Finally, the ultimate way the Lord communicates with us rationally is through the Word of God. So even though there could be "words of wisdom" gifts, they are all subject to and must be tested with the filter of the Word of God, the Bible. Here is the ultimate manifestation of the gifts of the Holy Spirit:

> Let the word of Christ dwell in you richly, teaching and admonishing one another in all wisdom, singing psalms and hymns and spiritual songs, with thankfulness in your hearts to God. (Colossians 3:16)

Introduction to
Volumes II, III, and IV

This was the first volume of the *21st Century Burning Bushes* series.

- *Volume II will cover the Burning Bushes of Science and Technology.*

The technological advances of the last one hundred years have been nothing short of miraculous. Knowledge has increased and is increasing at an unprecedented rate! This is predicted in Daniel 12:4:

> But you, Daniel, roll up and seal the words of the scroll until the time of the end. Many will go here and there to increase knowledge.

Movement has also increased as we witnessed an explosion in transportation technologies.

What we are witnessing today in terms of digitization and automation is nothing short of "magic." Of course, I am referring to a famous quote bey Arthur C. Clarke: "Any sufficiently advanced technology is indistinguishable from magic."

We are living in what is called the fourth industrial revolution. It is the information age par excellence. Every aspect of our lives is governed by technology, especially digital technology and particularly artificial intelligence (AI).

Digital transformation captures this: digital technology that is transforming all aspects of our lives.

There is also good news in that more recent advances in science have challenged the pervasive materialistic and neo-Darwinian worldview. The evidence of Intelligent Design is overwhelming. Honest atheistic materialists are in the defensive, and many of them have found faith and converted to Christianity—based on the indisputable scientific evidence.

So, this volume will treat the whole ecosystem of digital technology and science and provide a solid scientific and biblical perspective—holistically. Science and religion—especially Christianity—not only do not contradict each other; rather, science evidentially reinforces the Intelligent Design by our Creator, who is just amazing and worthy of our worship! He is the ultimate scientist, and all scientific research and endeavors are nothing but our feeble attempts to discover the laws and workings of His incredible creation!

- *Volume III will cover the Burning Bushes of Culture, Morality, and the Kingdom.*

There are startling social and cultural trends in the twenty-first century. It is a Burning Bush that is challenging and even shaking what it means to be a Christian even what it means to be human in modern society. Morality itself is undergoing unprecedented transformation. The twentieth and twenty-first centuries witnessed unbelievable evil atrocities, genocides, and wars. The rise of fascism and communism and their destructive influences have caused immeasurable harm to innocent humans. Different forms of slavery as well as child trafficking are very much alive and active. Abortion alone has murdered more than one billion innocent babies!

The sexual revolutions started in the twentieth century, and it got only worse with the emergence of the perverse LGBTQIA+ agenda and the even stranger transgender anomaly. The very meaning of what it means to be a man or woman is being challenged with inconceivable harm for families and especially children.

Christian Western culture is surrounded by so many challenges—including globalist One World Government— and increasingly trends to promote a One World Religion. Though more subtle and incremental, the erosion of our freedoms and government control is approaching those of the fascist and communist regimes of the previous century. These are precursors to the imminent end and conclusion of history.

The social and cultural trends of what is the norm in accepting others, what is acceptable in the society and especially modern Christian context is becoming accentuated. The Christian church and society is becoming weak and polarized. Normal Christian values that were common in the first half of the twentieth century are now deemed politically incorrect, "offensive," and even "terroristic."

Volume 3 will expose these Cultural, Social, and Moral trends.

- *Volume IV will cover the Burning Bushes of End-Time Signs and Wonders.*

Volume 4 focuses on the amazing convergence of many events, signs, and wonders leading to the potential conclusion of human history. The disclosure of UFO by the US government, the reality of abductions, supernatural manifestations, and the amazing discoveries of a potentially different—real and factual—history of humanity are probably a precursor to the end of the age. There is a nefarious plan that is being executed—with a concurrent deception looking elsewhere to explain the existence of the intelligent human race and the potential salvation of humanity through extraterrestrial. It is a deception of far-reaching consequences—dealing with the essential battles for the souls of humanity between God and Satan.

We are living in a supernatural universe filled with signs and wonders. However, the manifestations of these signs and wonders are entirely unpredictable. Among those is also the divisions and falling away and apostasy of the Church. At the same time, the gospel is preached to many nations. Our Lord predicted those and described the pangs of childbirth that will precede the end of history. That is the focus of this volume.

While many of the Burning Bushes are also End-Times Burning Bushes, this volume delves deeply into more nonconventional but critical "fringe" topics, such as Unidentified Flying Objects (UFOs or UAPs), Megalithic Structures, Ancient Civilizations, Portals, Crop Circles, Cattle Mutilations, Elongated Skulls, Abductions for hybrids, Giants and the Nephilim. It also covers the state of Israel and the interpretations of the book of Revelation. The last chapter is about the New Heaven and New Earth: the ultimate Burning Bush and the glorious culmination of history.

These four volumes attempt to connect the dots. The spectrum of topics is many and often covered under categories such as end-times, apologetics, fringe topics, doctrine—to name a few. But in fact, they are all Burning Bushes. I pray as you read these pages, you will turn around and see what these strange manifestations are all about.

We are living in very strange times. Are these the precursor to the return of our Lord? Feels that way, but who knows! No matter when we are living, we need to turn around and examine what appears to be unusual, and the Lord will then reveal His truth and plans to us!

He is still speaking to us through Burning Bushes.

Printed in the USA
CPSIA information can be obtained
at www.ICGtesting.com
LVHW071941220823
755992LV00007B/16

9 781662 939891